Sherman's March
to the Sea

CIVIL WAR CAMPAIGNS AND COMMANDERS SERIES

Under the General Editorship of Grady McWhiney

PUBLISHED

Sherman's March to the Sea

John F. Marszalek
Giles Distinguished Professor Emeritus
Mississippi State University

MCWHINEY FOUNDATION PRESS
MCMURRY UNIVERSITY
ABILENE, TEXAS

Library of Congress Cataloging-in-Publication Data

Marszalek, John F., 1939-
    Sherman's march to the sea / by John F. Marszalek.—1st ed.
       p. cm.—(Civil War campaigns and commanders series)
    Includes bibliographical references (p.) and index.
    ISBN 1-893114-16-3 (pbk.)
    1. Sherman's March to the Sea. 2. Sherman, William T.
(William Tecumseh), 1820-1891. I. Title. II. Series.

      E476.69.M37 2005
      973.7'378—dc22   2005000306
                                       CIP

McWhiney Foundation Press
McMurry University, Box 637
Abilene, Texas 79697
(325) 793-4682
www.mcwhiney.org.

Printed in the United States of America

ISBN 1-893114-16-3
10 9 8 7 6 5 4 3 2 1

Book Designed by Rosenbohm Graphic Design

For Vincent P. De Santis
Distinguished historian, mentor, and friend

"Sherman's March to the Sea, like the
retreat of Xenophon and his ten thousand
Greeks, will, through all ages, arouse
the enthusiasm of the schoolboy, the
fervor of the orator, and the admiration
of the stratcgist."

—Chauncey Depew,
In Memoriam William T. Sherman (1892)

"There can be little doubt that Sherman's
actions towards a proud and almost defenseless
people left a heritage which lasted far longer
than it might otherwise have lasted."

—John B. Walters, *Merchant of Terror, General
General Sherman and Total War* (1973)

CONTENTS

CAMPAIGNS AND COMMANDERS SERIES

Map Key

Geography

 Trees

 Marsh

 Fields

 Strategic Elevations

 Rivers

 Tactical Elevations

 Fords

 Orchards

 Political Boundaries

Human Construction

 Bridges

 Railroads

 Tactical Towns

 Strategic Towns

 Buildings

Church

Roads

Military

 Union Infantry

 Confederate Infantry

 Cavalry

 Artillery

Headquarters

 Encampments

 Fortifications

 Permanant Works

Hasty Works

Obstructions

 Engagements

Warships

 Gunboats

 Casemate Ironclad

 Monitor

 Tactical Movements

 Strategic Movements

Maps by
Donald S. Frazier, Ph.D.
Abilene, Texas

MAPS

BIOGRAPHICAL SKETCHES

PHOTOGRAPHS

Photographs from the Library of Congress, the National Archives, and Francis Miller's
Photographic History of the Civil War.

Sherman's March to the Sea

INTRODUCTION

Most Americans have heard of it, but few know the actual facts about it. Sherman's march to the sea is part of American mythology, imprinted on the public mind through motion pictures like "Gone With the Wind." It is an essential part of "The Lost Cause" view of the Civil War, the perception that, while the South lost the war, it was more virtuous than the victorious North, whose basic immorality was exemplified in the person of William T. Sherman and his allegedly brutish march to the sea.

The historical reality is much more complicated than the myth, and this book is an attempt to demonstrate that. Warfare is never simple, and, more often than not when human beings come into conflict, there is no clear distinction between heroes and villains. So it was with this cataclysmic event which so defined the direction of the Civil War. It was part of the development of modern warfare, the ascendance of the idea that war does not consist simply of armies fighting other armies on battlefields, but rather of societies battling each other through calculated destruction in order to break the other's will. Sherman's march to the sea was not the application of senseless brutality for its own sake; it was a well-planned attempt to break the will of the Confederacy and bring the Civil War to a more rapid end.

The central figure in the implementation of this warfare was William Tecumseh Sherman. Much of this book, therefore, focuses on him. He was a brilliant and purposeful man whose experiences in life led him to a warfare of destructiveness. Far from being a South-hating brute, he had great affection for the region, having lived in the South much of his life and made many friends among its people. His major purpose for marching to the sea was not to brutalize but to end the war as quickly as possible with the least loss of life.

Sherman began his famous march in mid-November 1864 after his capture of Atlanta in the early fall of that year. By that time, he was, next to Ulysses S. Grant, already the Union's leading general. He had fought at First Bull Run (Manassas), served a tempestuous tour of duty in Kentucky and Missouri, been the hero of Shiloh, successfully governed Memphis, played essential military roles at Vicksburg and Chattanooga, and conducted the Meridian Campaign through Mississippi.

His capture of Atlanta had solidified his fame, coming as it did during the 1864 presidential campaign when it gave Lincoln's reelection effort an essential boost. Quickly, however, Sherman had to decide on his next move. He did not believe that he could remain in the interior of Georgia indefinitely. His decision: cut himself and his huge army off from his supply base and bring war home to the Confederate populace by marching through the heartland of Georgia to the Atlantic Ocean.

The book that follows begins with Sherman in Atlanta in the fall of 1864 and discusses how he made his decision to undertake the march and how he organized his army to accomplish it. The book then describes what the march was like—to the

Sherman and his commanders after the fall of Atlanta.

soldiers who made the journey and the white Confederates and the black slaves who found themselves in its path. The book tells of the destruction that took place during the march and assesses responsibility. It discusses the armed conflict during the march and Sherman's reversion to "soft war" once the Union army captured Savannah. Finally, the book ends with a discussion of the impact of the march on Sherman's reputation.

This book would have been impossible without the published insights of a variety of earlier historians. Their names and publications appear in the Further Readings section. The following historians read earlier drafts of this manuscript and offered important suggestions: Anne J. Bailey, Michael B. Ballard, Albert Castel, Mark Grimsley, Charles D. Lowery, William E. Parrish, and Craig L. Symonds. My wife, Jeanne A. Marszalek, provided her usual perceptive comments.

Over forty years ago, I took my first class from Vincent P. De Santis at the University of Notre Dame. Later, under his direction, I wrote my doctoral dissertation (on William T. Sherman and the press). From that time to the present, this distinguished historian has challenged and inspired me in more ways than he realizes. I look forward to many more years of learning from him and enjoying his friendship. It is with gratitude and pleasure that I dedicate this book to him.

1

THE DECISION TO MARCH

William T. Sherman captured Atlanta on September 2, 1864, concluding the campaign that would ensure his historical fame. The city at one time during the war was home to over twenty thousand people, having grown from ten thousand inhabitants in the late 1850s. Only three thousand residents remained in Atlanta when Sherman arrived. "Houses were shattered and torn in every shape that can be imagined," an Indiana doctor marching with Sherman recorded in his diary. No longer the prosperous railroad and manufacturing center it had once been, Atlanta was now a casualty of war.

Despite this victory, by the end of September, Sherman found himself chasing John Bell Hood's Army of Tennessee over the same terrain recently wrested from that same Confederate army, then under Joseph E. Johnston. Hood sought to cut the Western and Atlantic Railroad that served as Sherman's thin supply line throughout the Atlanta Campaign and which remained the sole source of support for his army.

Sherman could not allow Hood to disrupt his supplies, so he purposefully followed the Confederate, growing more frustrated with every passing day and mile. Wearing "his old round crowned black hat, pulled down over one ear, leaving the other out in the cold," as one Union soldier described it, Sherman was obviously exasperated. Hood "is eccentric," Sherman complained, "I cannot guess his movements as I could those of Johnston, who was a sensible man and only did sensible things." When one Union officer noted that the Confederate army stood only a short distance from where it had begun the Atlanta campaign the previous May, Sherman's frustration peaked.

WILLIAM TECUMSEH SHERMAN

William Tecumseh Sherman: Born in Lancaster, Ohio, in 1820, the son of Charles R. and Mary Sherman. At the age of nine, his father died, and he joined the family of Thomas Ewing, a neighbor and later prominent Whig politician. Ewing sent the young Sherman to the United States Military Academy when he was sixteen-years-old. Sherman graduated sixth out of a class of forty-two in 1840. His first military assignments sent him south: Florida, Alabama, and South Carolina. In 1847, while serving as a recruiting officer in Pittsburg, Sherman received orders for California. The three years he spent in the western state resulted in no Mexican War combat experience, though he did play an important role in the gold rush of 1849. During the early 1850s, Sherman held commissary posts in St. Louis and New Orleans, and from 1853 to 1857 he was a banker in San Francisco. The bank closed, and he spent the next several years failing at another bank position in New York City. Sherman's bad luck in civilian employment carried over to law and real estate businesses in Kansas. Extremely discouraged, Sherman tried to return to the army, but, instead became superintendent of the Louisiana Military Seminary in Alexandria, Louisiana. When secession came, he felt duty bound to return to the North. He briefly served as president of a St. Louis street railway company and, in June 1861, was appointed colonel of the 13th United States Infantry Regiment. At the battle of First Bull Run, he commanded a brigade and was

As was the case throughout the war, Sherman slept little, normally awaking at 3 or 4 A.M. In the field, the Union general ruminated during the night in front of flickering camp fires, sometimes even walking back and forth with the sentinel, carrying on extended conversations, while he considered his army's next move. George F. Cram of the 105th Illinois Infantry Regiment recalled Sherman visiting his regiment's camp for dinner in October, displaying an inability "to keep still a moment."

After much thought, Sherman decided that chasing after Hood made no sense. Protecting the railroad had become a waste of time and effort because it required too many soldiers

recognized for outstanding service. In the fall of 1861, the pressure of command in Kentucky caused him intense anxiety and depression. He was transferred to Missouri, but his commanding officer, Henry W. Halleck, sent him home in December 1861, among rumors fanned by newspapers, that the general was insane. In January 1862, Sherman was sent to train recruits in Missouri, but association with Ulysses S. Grant revived his military career. Sherman became a division commander under Grant at Shiloh and distinguished himself in combat, though he shared the blame for the Confederate surprise of Shiloh. He steadily rose in rank and influence. In the summer of 1862, Sherman became military governor of Memphis. His attack against a Confederate position at Chickasaw Bayou near Vicksburg failed in December, but Sherman retained Grant's respect and rose in rank with him. Sherman participated in the successful capture of Vicksburg in July 1863, helped to relieve the siege at Chattanooga in the fall, and led the successful Meridian Campaign in February 1864. When Grant moved to Washington as commanding general, Sherman gained command of the Union army in the West, and orchestrated the successful Atlanta campaign, the march across Georgia, and then through the Carolinas. When the war ended, despite his overly-generous peace terms to Confederate Gen. Joseph E. Johnston, Sherman was one of the world's admired generals. From 1865 to 1869, Sherman commanded troops in the western plains and when Grant became president in 1869, he became a commanding general, a post he held until his retirement in 1883. Sherman refused to run for the presidency on numerous occasions, most famously in 1884, and he spent his retirement involved in veterans affairs and Civil War history, one of the most popular men of his time. Sherman died in 1891 in New York City and is buried in St. Louis.

and kept the army on the defensive, susceptible to Confederate initiative. Sherman also knew that he could not stay in Atlanta for long without a supply line. He therefore decided to change his base, away from the isolated Georgia city, to some place along the coast where he could secure a source of supply from the Union fleet. He told Maj. Gen. George H. Thomas, as early as October 9, 1864, of his decision to "destroy all the [rail]road below Chattanooga, including Atlanta, and make for the sea-coast." He wrote his wife Ellen just twelve days later, "This Army is now ready to march to Mobile, Savannah or Charleston, and I am practicing them in the art of foraging and they take to it like ducks to water."

The decision to march to the coast did not come to Sherman suddenly in the still of some Georgia night. It resulted from a life-time of military and civilian experiences and the turmoil of Civil War conflict. He had been gradually preparing himself for this advance since the early days of his childhood, and the direction of the war had pushed him toward this momentous decision.

As a boy of sixteen, Sherman received an appointment to the United States Military Academy at West Point and spent four years of alternating boredom and contentment. A bright lad, he graduated sixth in his 1840 class, losing two places because of demerits. While at the Academy, he was exposed to viewpoints that influenced his later method of conducting war. His moral philosophy class read James Kent's *Commentaries on American Law*, which, among other points, argued that war caused a dissolution of morality and was fought not simply between two opposing armies but between two societies. After graduation, when Sherman found himself in Florida battling the Seminole Indians, he noted the same thing. The U.S. Army could not simply defeat the fighters; it had to put down the entire society which supported them. Similarly, the Seminoles did not attack the U.S. Army alone; they battled the entire white society backing the soldiers. In theory and practice,

GEORGE H. THOMAS

George H. Thomas: Born in Southampton County, Virginia, in 1816, Thomas remained loyal to the Union despite his southern birth. He graduated from the United States Military Academy, finishing twelfth out of a class of forty-two in 1840, the same year that William T. Sherman finished sixth. Thomas joined the artillery and served in the Seminole War in Florida and with distinction in the Mexican War battles of Monterrey and Buena Vista. He then became an artillery and cavalry instructor at West Point and, during the late 1850s, served under later Confederate generals Albert Sidney Johnston and Robert E. Lee in Texas. He also served with William J. Hardee and John Bell Hood. Thomas was on a one year leave of absence because of an inquiry when secession came. Despite receiving an offer from the Virginia governor to become chief of ordnance, he made the difficult personal decision to retain his United States Army commission. His family never forgave him for his decision, and refused to have anything to do with Thomas for the rest of their lives. At first he served in the eastern theater of the war, holding a colonelship in the Shenandoah Valley. Promoted to brigadier general in August 1861, Thomas moved to Kentucky and was successful at Mill Springs and later became a division commander at Shiloh. Promoted to major general in late April 1862, he participated in the siege of Corinth and the battles of Perryville and Stones River. Thomas gained his greatest fame at the battle of Chickamauga when, as a corps commander, he repelled repeated Confederate assaults and saved the Union army. He acquired the name "The Rock of Chickamauga." Thomas became commander of the Army of the Cumberland in October 1863; and it was his men who, without orders, stormed Missionary Ridge at Chattanooga. He was the solid middle of Sherman's Atlanta Campaign; and, while Sherman marched to the sea, Thomas demolished Hood's Army of Tennessee at Nashville. Thomas remained in command in Tennessee until 1867 when he moved to the Pacific Coast. He died of a stroke in 1870. He was a heavy-set man whose nicknames "Old Tom," "Slow Trot," and "Pap Thomas" indicated his reputation for slowness. Grant found his deliberateness exasperating as did Sherman, though the latter linked him with Grant as one of the greatest generals of the war.

therefore, Sherman was exposed to the fact that war was society against society, not simply army against army.

After further tours of army service in St. Augustine, Florida, Fort Morgan, Alabama, and Fort Moultrie in Charleston, South Carolina, Sherman continued his military education in California during the Mexican War of the late 1840s. Helping to organize his unit's supplies for the 198 day trip by ship around South America taught the young officer the importance of logistics to military operations. Sherman later noted that civilian migrants reached California overland from the East, without any sure supply source. The wagon trains of men, women, and children struck out across the great plains and the imposing mountains, cutting themselves off from the outside world to live off the land. The pioneers fought off Native Americans, and survived. If civilians could do it, he reasoned, why could a trained army not also depend on its own initiative instead of conventional supply bases and systems?

In the early 1850s, Sherman held army logistical positions in St. Louis and New Orleans. From 1853 to 1857, he was a San Francisco banker, a Kansas entrepreneur, and a military seminary superintendent in Louisiana. In all these roles, Sherman had similar experiences; he realized no matter what the profession, no matter where the locale, society's cohesion depended on secure patterns of supply. Disrupt such patterns, and society becomes disoriented and cannot maintain its unity.

When Sherman re-entered the army in 1861, however, he embraced a more traditional military philosophy. Like all his military compatriots on both sides, he was a soldier of conservative beliefs, whose primary West Point heritage taught him that professionals fought wars divorced from society. Armies did not accost civilians because such actions were not professionally proper. Thus, when Sherman marched his brigade from Washington, through the Virginia countryside, to the site of the battle of First Bull Run (Manassas), he condemned pillaging and tried to keep Union soldiers from indulging in even the least instance of it. He became frustrated in his effort. He complained bitterly that "No goths or vandals ever had less respect for the lives & property of friends and foes" than Union soldiers.

Despite the predominance of such conservative ideas, the insights gained from the Seminole War, the West Point moral philosophy class, and other military and professional experiences remained in the back of the general's mind. In July 1862, he became the military governor of Memphis, and his conservative ideals were further challenged. Sherman expressed shock when a Memphis pastor refused to include in his service the traditional prayer for the president of the United States. Confederate slave holders exasperated him when they demanded that the Union army track down their run-away slaves. The general fought a losing battle against individuals who smuggled goods out of the city and continued to publish a newspaper, two activities, he believed, aided the Confederate military. It angered Sherman when Southerners "burn[ed] their cotton, their houses, anything cheerfully at the order of a single Southern Dragoon, but if one of our men burns a rail, steals a chicken, robs a garden . . . they raise a hue & cry."

Most of all, the Union general was appalled when Confederate guerrillas attacked his soldiers, harassed area Unionists, and even fired on passenger boats carrying women and children down the Mississippi River. "When one nation is at war with another, all the people of one are enemies of the other," Sherman proclaimed in Memphis. "We are not going to chase through the canebreaks and swamps the individuals who did the deeds," he said in an obvious flashback to the Seminoles, "but will visit punishment upon the adherents of that cause which employs such agents." And perhaps even more apocalyptically, Sherman's wife Ellen declared: "I hope this may be not only a war of emancipation but [also] of extermination & that all under the influence of the foul fiend may be driven like Swine into the Sea. May we carry fire & sword into their states till not one habitation is left standing."

As Sherman's perception of war changed, he slowly began to act in new ways. When guerrillas kept firing on river boats despite his conventional military efforts to stop them, he adopted a new approach in the late summer and early fall of 1862. Sherman's army destroyed the village of Randolph, Tennessee, near the site of one such attack. He warned Memphians that, for every Unionist bothered, ten Confederate families would be expelled in retaliation, an act which moved William T. Sherman away from the role of a traditional warrior. Indeed, the Civil War itself was moving inexorably toward a harsher totality on both sides, and Sherman's experiences pushed him to the forefront of this phenomenon. In May 1863 he still made an important distinction, however, "Of course I expect & do take corn, bacon, horses, mules and everything to support an army, and don't object much to the using [of] fences for firewood, but this universal burning and wanton destruction of private property is not justifiable in war."

In December 1862, Sherman used conventional tactics in an unsuccessful attempt to dislodge Confederate forces from the Walnut Hills at Chickasaw Bayou just north of Vicksburg, the major Confederate stronghold on the Mississippi River. Later, when he became part of Ulysses S. Grant's successful July 1863 capture of that Gibraltar of the West, he promised to treat "my old pupils & friends" who were inside the city "with kindness," but "until they lay down their arms, and submit to the rightful authority of their Government, they must make no appeal to me for mercy or favors." He opposed, but went along with, Grant's brilliant plan of marching the Union Army down the Louisiana side of the Mississippi River, south of Vicksburg, then ferrying it across the river to the Mississippi side, eventually placing the Union army between John C. Pemberton's Confederates at Vicksburg and Joseph E. Johnston's army in Jackson, Mississippi. Grant defeated one and then the other force, while at the same time operating on an unsure supply line. Sherman filed away for future reference the concrete example of an army living off the countryside.

At this time, despite his earlier leveling of Randolph, Tennessee, Sherman still disdainfully condemned the destruction that occurred in Jackson, Mississippi, in mid-July 1863. He wrote disgustedly: "The enemy burned nearly all the handsome dwellings, round about the Town, because they gave us shelter, or to light up the ground, to prevent night attacks. He also set fire to a chief block of stores in which were commissary supplies, and our men in spite of guards have widened the circle of fire so that Jackson, once the pride and boast of Mississippi is now a ruined Town." Union and Confederate soldiers routinely burned and pillaged, and Sherman did not like it. "The only possible remedy" Southerners had, however, "was to stop [the] war," he insisted.

More conventional war lay in Sherman's future, such as participation in lifting the Confederate siege at Chattanooga, and then conducting his own dramatic Atlanta campaign. In February 1864, however, he finally put into practice his ideas about destructive war. Sherman convinced Grant and Henry W. Halleck, his superiors, that he should march an army from Vicksburg through Jackson to Meridian, Mississippi. He planned to ravage the countryside as he proceeded, his aim to neutralize the Confederate regular army and the guerrillas creating havoc along the Mississippi River. If these partisans had no safe havens, they would no longer be a threat, and if the Confederate regular army was chased away, Sherman would not have to waste troops in garrison duty.

Sherman maintained the affection for Southerners that he had developed during his pre-war years of army service and civilian life in the South. Therefore, he hoped that a war against southern property would negate the necessity for a combat of killing and maiming. He told his daughter in July 1861 not to "get in the habit of calling [Southerners] hard names of Rebels, Traitors, but remember how easy it is for people to become deceived and drawn step by step, till death and destruction are upon them." He later told this same daughter that in every one of the battles he fought during the war, he contested "some of the very families in whose homes I used to spend some happy days" while a young soldier in the South. "Of course I must fight them when the time comes," he realized, "but whenever a result can be accomplished without battle I prefer it." Sherman wanted to stop killing and wounding his friends and looked to destroying their property as a more efficient and humane way to convince them to stop fighting.

The Meridian plan was as simple as it was revolutionary. Sherman "would make this war as severe as possible and make no symptoms of [being] tire[d], till the South begs for

HENRY W. HALLECK

Henry W. Halleck: Born in Westernville, New York, in 1814, Halleck attended Union College where he made Phi Beta Kappa, and the United States Military Academy where he graduated third in his class of thirty-one in 1839. A member of the West Point faculty, Halleck later helped build fortifications in New York harbor, and traveled to France to study that nation's military organization and defense systems. In 1844, Halleck wrote *Report on the Means of National Defense,* and later gave a series of lectures that were published as the immensely influential *Elements of Military Art and Science.* Halleck then translated into English Antoine Henri Jomini's 4 volume *Vie Politique et Militaire de Napoleon.* Halleck and Sherman traveled to California together during the Mexican War, where he held a host of military government positions, including secretary of state. When California became a state, Halleck remained there as a military engineer but simultaneously held civilian positions including an attorney in San Francisco and a manager of a quicksilver mine. He resigned his army commission in 1854 to concentrate on his civilian legal and business activities which made him one of San Francisco's richest men. Halleck was a leader of the state's militia when secession came. He returned to the United mercy. Indeed I know and you know," he told Grant as early as September 1863, "that the end would be reached quicker by such course, than by any seeming yielding on our part." Sherman planned to divide his twenty thousand man force into two wings for the march through the Mississippi countryside. At the same time, William Sooy Smith and seven thousand cavalrymen were to leave Collierville, Tennessee, and proceed south through eastern Mississippi to meet the main force at Meridian. Sherman ordered his soldiers to strip down to the bare essentials, so they could move as quickly as possible; and he worked to organize every detail of the movement.

Although convinced that such a war of destruction was the most efficient way to end the conflict quickly, he worried about the reaction of the Southerners. He wrote a public letter that

States Army as a major general and, although Winfield Scott hoped he would be his replacement as commanding general, Halleck instead replaced John C. Fremont as head of the Department of Missouri. Halleck brought order to the region and received promotion to command of the Department of the Mississippi. He then oversaw Grant's victories at Forts Henry and Donelson and at Shiloh and then massed troops in the region to take Corinth in May 1862, although it took him a month to do so. In July 1862, Lincoln named Halleck commander of all Union armies, and the general moved to Washington. Halleck demonstrated the ability to administer the army, but did not take to the field to command any part of the army directly. In March 1864, when Lincoln named Grant the new commanding general, Halleck became the first chief of staff in American military history. In April 1865, with the war over, Halleck was sent to command the Department of Virginia and the Army of the James, and in August 1865 he became commander of the Military Division of the Pacific. In 1869, Halleck moved to Louisville, Kentucky, to take command of the Military Division of the South. He died there in 1872 and is buried in Brooklyn, New York. Nicknamed "Old Brains" by his soldiers after the capture of Corinth, Halleck was never an aggressive military leader. Sherman admired him until the conflict's last days, even when Halleck accused Sherman of collaborating with the enemy in his peace terms with Joseph E. Johnston. Most other Union officials came to have a low opinion of him earlier than Sherman, and Lincoln called Halleck "little more than a first rate clerk." Halleck was an excellent administrator but, because of physical and psychological factors, had difficulty rising above mundane matters to provide the inspiring leadership the times required.

pointed out how the British had previously waged such a war against Irish civilians. Sherman also justified himself by insisting that since the enemy used horses, mules, food, forage, and all sorts of other supplies to wage war, he not only had the right but also the duty to confiscate or destroy such materials. Those who insisted on rebelling against "a Government so mild and just as ours was in peace," he said, deserved harsh punishment. Once they stopped fighting, however, he promised "all gentleness and forbearance."

He told Sooy Smith the same thing. "Take freely the horses, mules, cattle, &c. of the hostile or indifferent inhabitants, and let them all understand that if from design or weakness they permit their country to be used by the public enemy[,] they must bear the expenses of the troops sent to expel them . . . But in counties where people have acted properly," he added, "a broad distinction should be made." Clearly, Sherman saw the confiscation or destruction of property not only as a military means but also as a means to end the war quickly in a more humane way than through conventional battle. But he did not call for indiscriminate destruction. The campaign should focus on those who needed encouragement to cease fighting; once they quit, destruction would end.

Sherman and his twenty thousand man army departed Vicksburg on February 3, 1864. The left wing, the XVI Corps, marched under Stephen Hurlbut, while the right one, the XVII Corps, was under James B. McPherson. Thirteen hundred cavalry acted as a screen for the main columns. When Sherman's force left Vicksburg, the army's supply base was lost.

As they marched, Sherman's troopers scavenged off the land, gathering whatever would feed their army, and thereby denying resources to the Confederate army and guerrillas. The soldiers damaged and destroyed barns and houses, stores and shops, railroad tracks and bridges. They took farm animals and produce, and freed slaves. The Union army made it clear to civilians that the war would be costly if continued, and the

Confederacy stood helpless in the face of this juggernaut. Confederate Gen. Leonidas Polk had two divisions of infantry in Meridian, but his two divisions of cavalry, including Nathan Bedford Forrest's horsemen, were dispersed throughout Mississippi. Polk and his scattered troops offered only minimal opposition. Mississippi civilians were at the mercy of Sherman.

Sherman arrived in Meridian on February 14, 1864, to find that the city's defenders had fled to the east. He momentarily thought about pursuing Polk's Confederate army into Alabama, but since Sooy Smith had not arrived as scheduled, he decided against it. (As it happened, Smith did not leave Tennessee until February 11, and on February 21 and 22, Forrest drove him back to Memphis after engagements in West Point and Okolona.) Sherman's decision not to pursue Polk was not surprising. The Union general was less interested in killing Confederate soldiers than in destroying Confederate material and morale. After giving his soldiers a day of rest, Sherman put them to work wrecking miles of railroad in all directions from Meridian. The soldiers then destroyed the war-making potential of the city itself.

The Meridian Campaign accomplished exactly what Sherman had hoped it would—the wholesale destruction of the infrastructure of the society supporting Confederate forces, without killing a large number of soldiers or civilians. At the same time, the operation demonstrated the weakness of the Confederate military. Confederate leaders were unable to use troops to protect civilians against such an incursion. The Confederacy was a hollow shell, as Sherman later stated. The Union army could march through the region without opposition, and feed its men off the countryside at the same time. Sherman could fight such a war with a minimum loss of life, and be successful. He believed he could convince southern civilians not to continue supporting a war that had become so physically and psychologically devastating. The Meridian Campaign offered the South an important lesson; it convinced

Sherman that administering a campaign against civilians could end the war quickly. Historian Buckley T. Foster is correct in labeling this expedition the "dress rehearsal" for what Sherman was later to do in Georgia.

In consequence of his success in the Meridian Campaign, Sherman quite naturally decided to institute destructive war. Unlike most other Civil War generals (with the conspicuous exception of Grant) Sherman willingly left traditional ways behind to try new approaches. His march to the sea, while not revolutionary in the history of warfare, had an impact on the Civil War and on the history of the nation unlike any other event in the American past. Sherman realized that defeating Confederate armies would not suffice; he had to destroy the main Confederate strength: the morale and will of its people.

2
ORGANIZING THE MARCH

It was one thing for Sherman to decide what to do, quite another to convince his superiors, and yet another to plan and organize the effort. After all, he still had to contend with John Bell Hood. If Sherman turned his back on Hood and gave the Confederate a free hand in Georgia and, even more importantly in Tennessee, Hood might well march north, unimpeded, and create an enormous military and morale problem for the Federals. To avoid such a calamity, Sherman instructed his subordinate George H. Thomas to defeat Hood. Sherman was convinced, as he told Grant in October 1864 that "Old Tom" was "better suited to the emergency than any man I have." Thomas could handle Hood from his base in Nashville and provide Sherman with the freedom to proceed with destructive and psychological operations in Georgia. Once the Union army reached the ocean, Sherman could turn northward to link up with Grant. As Sherman's troops marched across Georgia, the Union general planned to keep his eye on Robert E. Lee and

JOHN BELL HOOD

John Bell Hood: Born in Owingsville, Kentucky, in 1831, Hood graduated from the United States Military Academy in 1853, forty-fourth out of a class of fifty-two. Between 1853 and 1857, he served in California and Texas, and in 1857 took part in the Indian wars in the Lone

Star State. When secession came, Hood resigned his commission in the United States Army and became a captain of Confederate cavalry, and then in the fall was promoted to Colonel of the 4th Texas Regiment. A part of the Army of Northern Virginia, Hood moved steadily through the ranks and reached the status of major general in October 1862. He performed admirably as division commander at Antietam and Fredericksburg under Gen. James Longstreet. Hood was particularly devoted to Lee. At Gettysburg, the Confederate general suffered a wound which crippled one arm, and at Chickamauga, as a corps commander, he lost a leg. Though crippled, Hood commanded a corps under Joseph E. Johnston during the Atlanta campaign, where Hood was critical of Johnston throughout the fighting. When Jefferson Davis fired Johnston in anger after Sherman's army reached the outskirts of Atlanta, Hood took over. Following what Hood believed to be the example of Lee and the desires of Davis, the new commander went on the offensive, only to suffer a series of severe repulses in the Atlanta area. Sherman then flanked him out of the city and took over Atlanta in September 1864. Hood then attempted to cut Sherman's supply line to Chattanooga by destroying railroad tracks, but when Sherman decided to march across Georgia, Sherman himself gave orders to have the railroad destroyed. George H. Thomas, to whom Sherman assigned the task of thwarting Hood, accomplished this mission spectacularly at Nashville in December 1864. As at Atlanta, Hood's offensive operations led his army to resounding defeat. After Nashville, the Army of Tennessee was a fatally crippled unit, and Jefferson Davis's recall of Johnston came too late. In the post-war period, Hood married, and his wife had eleven children in ten years. The Hood family lived in New Orleans, where Hood was a merchant, but severe financial reverses doomed his chances for monetary security. Sherman and Hood were friendly after the war, and Sherman even tried to help his former enemy sell his personal papers in order to alleviate Hood's money problems. Together with his wife and one of his children, Hood died from yellow fever in 1879. Hood was a hard fighting division commander, but proved a failure as leader of an army.

the Army of Northern Virginia then battling Grant for Richmond.

Union leaders were not sure Sherman's decision was the right move. Joseph Hooker, who was furious at Sherman for not giving him command of the Army of the Tennessee after James B. McPherson was killed during the Atlanta Campaign, ridiculed the whole idea. "Sherman is crazy," Hooker said in early December 1864, "he has no more judgment than a child." Even Grant never fully accepted Sherman's reasoning, wishing instead that his colleague would crush Hood before the march began. Still, Grant gave in to Sherman. The two generals had developed such a close relationship that Grant trusted his associate despite his own misgivings. Once Grant said yes, Chief of Staff Henry W. Halleck agreed, too. Secretary of War Edwin M. Stanton reluctantly agreed to the plan, which meant President Abraham Lincoln had also dropped his opposition. Sherman achieved the first part of his task. His superiors had granted him permission to march to the sea. He was confident his men could make it, but there were no guarantees. In fact, Sherman's army could very well be stymied in Georgia with disastrous results. The Union high command had every reason to be worried.

Having received permission, Sherman proceeded with his plans. In late September and October he assigned George H. Thomas and the IV and XIII Corps, some 22,000 men, to Nashville in order to keep an eye on Hood. Thomas gathered another 33,000 men from as far away as Missouri to reach a maximum strength of 55,000 men. Hood marched into Tuscumbia/Florence, Alabama at the end of October and remained there for three weeks. Hood had only 30,600 fighting men. Meanwhile, Sherman organized 62,000 of his healthiest soldiers for his own invading force, sending the sick and unfit back to Chattanooga along with unneeded supplies. Then Sherman did the unthinkable. The general who had spent the Atlanta Campaign obsessively defending the railroad which

EDWIN M. STANTON

Edwin M. Stanton: Born in Steubenville, Ohio, in 1814, Stanton had to leave school at the age of eleven to work in a bookstore to help his family survive the death of his father. Stanton took every opportunity to study on his own and then, from 1831 to 1833, he attended Kenyon

College. Stanton moved to Columbus, Ohio, and was admitted to the bar in 1836 after studies in a local law office. He gained national fame in Pittsburg as counsel for the state of Pennsylvania, serving in that post from 1849 to 1856. Stanton next became special federal counsel in some California land fraud cases, catapulting into the attorney generalship during the last days of James Buchanan's presidential administration. In the 1860 presidential election, although Stanton was an anti-slaveryite, he backed southern Democratic candidate John C. Breckinridge. When Lincoln took office and his first secretary of war proved to be incompetent, the president called on Stanton despite the famous lawyer's open criticism of the administration. Stanton took office in January 1862 and vigorously attacked the waste and mismanagement in the war department. He was an unflinching organizer, willing to oppose anyone, no matter their station, in order to bring organization to the Union war effort. Stanton enforced the controversial draft laws; limited the press; pushed for the use of black soldiers; and did whatever he thought necessary to prosecute the war. Stanton and Lincoln worked well together because the president was willing to ignore Stanton's eccentricities. When Lincoln was assassinated, the unfounded rumor started (and is still believed by some to the present day) that Stanton was part of the assassination conspiracy. During Reconstruction, the quarrel between Stanton, his "Radical Republican" allies, and President Andrew Johnson resulted in a constitutional crisis. Stanton resigned in May 1868 and received an appointment to the Supreme Court when Grant gained the presidency. He died in December 1869, four days after the completion of his Senate confirmation. Stanton was a no-nonsense administrator who gained numerous enemies because of his blunt determination to do his job effectively. He played a major role in the Union victory in the Civil War.

supplied his troops now destroyed that same railroad over its entire length from Chattanooga to Atlanta. To ensure that Washington did not change its mind and try to stop his opera-

Sherman ordering the cutting of telegraph lines, severing his only communication link with Union leaders.

tion, Sherman cut his telegraph communications. It was "like Cortez destroying his ships," an aide said, "that thoughts of retreat might not enter the minds of his men."

Sherman never thought of retreat; he had only one path: across Georgia toward the sea. "They are at my mercy," he reassured his superiors in Washington, "Do not be anxious about me. I am all right." Sherman intentionally cut himself off from the outside world for another reason as well; to keep reporters away. He convinced himself that one of the reasons for the success of Meridian had been the news blackout. During the Meridian Campaign the press was unable to publish any information helpful to the enemy, which Sherman believed had been the case earlier in the war.

Sherman replicated the organization that had worked so well during the Meridian Campaign. He established two wings of infantry with screening cavalry, convinced that such a formation allowed him to cover a wide front and destroy a large area. Should an unseen enemy try to attack his force, the

Sherman and his commanders: 1) O.O. Howard; 2) John A. Logan; 3) William B. Hazen; 4) William T. Sherman; 5) Jefferson C. Davis; 6) Henry W. Slocum; 7) Joseph A. Mower; 8) Frank P. Blair, Jr.

screening cavalry would send out a warning, and the two wings could quickly respond. Sherman realized that Hood would be busy with Thomas in Tennessee, and he also knew that the Confederates had only a sprinkling of other troops in the region. Not accidentally, however, his cavalry kept a special lookout for Robert E. Lee and any units from the Army of Northern Virginia. The fear of Lee merging with Hood was a constant Union concern. While Lee never remained far from Sherman's mind as he advanced through Georgia, in reality Sherman had no real reason to worry. Lee had all he could handle in Virginia.

Veteran soldiers made up the vast majority of Sherman's army, officers and enlisted men alike. Of his 238 regiments, 185 came from the Midwest, where most soldiers were farm boys. Despite three years of army service, some of them had not yet reached the voting age of twenty one. The seasoned veterans had participated in practically every major battle of the war. Historian Joseph Glatthaar described the soldiers as

looking "more like a mob than an army . . . unkempt, boister-
ous, seemingly [an] unruly lot," but "hardened and educated by
the war they had experienced." Historian Basil H. Liddell Hart
called them "probably the finest army of military 'workmen'
the modern world has seen."

The leaders of these youthful veterans were experienced
young men themselves. A vast majority of the lieutenants and
captains had worked their way up from the enlisted ranks. The
senior officers were also seasoned fighters. Oliver O. Howard,
a victim of Stonewall Jackson's flank attack at Chancellorsville
and also a veteran of Gettysburg and the Atlanta Campaign,
commanded the right (southern) wing, made up of the XV and
XVII Corps constituting the Army of the Tennessee. Henry W.
Slocum, another veteran of the major Eastern battles led the
left (northern) wing, made up of the XIV and XX Corps, once a
part of George H. Thomas's Army of the Cumberland, but now
called the Army of Georgia. Howard's corps commanders were
Peter J. Osterhaus (XV Corps), the highly successful foreign
born officer, and Frank P. Blair (XVII Corps), the equally successful political general. Slocum, meanwhile, had as his two
commanders, Jefferson C. Davis (XIV Corps), a man who had
led divisions at Murfreesboro, Chickamauga, and Atlanta; and
Alpheus S. Williams (XX Corps), who had done well in the East
before arriving in the West after Chickamauga. The controversial and flamboyant Judson Kilpatrick commanded the separate cavalry division.

In all, Sherman's two armies consisted of 62,000 infantry-
men, 5,000 cavalry men, 2,500 wagons, 16,000 horses and
mules, 600 ambulances, and sixty-five artillery pieces. If
strung out in a single column, Sherman's force would have
stretched for eighty miles.

Individual soldiers had to carry most of their necessities
because Sherman had forced his army to leave all but their
essentials behind. By this time in the war, however, veterans
knew how to travel light. Each man carried a rifle, a bayonet,

OLIVER OTIS HOWARD

Oliver Otis Howard: Born in Leeds, Maine, in 1830, Howard graduated from Bowdoin College in 1850 and then from the United States Military Academy in 1854. A member of the ordnance branch, Howard taught mathematics at the Academy. In May 1861, he was elected  colonel of the 3rd Maine Infantry Regiment; and, during the battle of First Bull Run, he was brigade commander. Despite a mediocre performance, Howard was promoted to brigadier general and participated in George McClellan's Peninsular Campaign, losing his right arm at Seven Pines. He then served as division commander at Antietam and Fredericksburg. Howard did not adequately protect his corps's flank at Chancellorsville, and Stonewall Jackson routed it. At Gettysburg, Howard's corps did not perform well again, but the general gained the thanks of Congress anyway for his excellent choice of fallback position. In the autumn of 1863, Howard's corps was part of Joseph Hooker's force sent to Chattanooga, and he commanded a corps during the Atlanta Campaign. When James B. McPherson died in battle, Sherman made Howard commander of the Army of the Tennessee, over Joe Hooker and John A. Logan, a talented political general. Howard commanded Sherman's right wing in the march to the sea and through the Carolinas. In May 1865, Howard became the first commissioner of the Freedmen's Bureau, and was a driving force in the establishment of Howard University for black students, serving as president from 1869 to 1874. He was superintendent of West Point, fought the Indians, and from 1886 to 1894 was commander of the Division of the East. In his retirement Howard helped establish Lincoln Memorial University in Tennessee for poor whites; and, in 1893, he received the Medal of Honor for his valor at Seven Pines. He died in Burlington, Vermont, in 1909. Known as the "Christian General," Howard was a religious man who attempted to express his piety in the way he lived his daily life and in his numerous humanitarian projects.

and eighty rounds of ammunition. Most carried a haversack, a canteen, tin cup, mess knife, a blanket rubberized on one side, and a tent fly made of canvas. Some men might have a knapsack and carry extra socks or a shirt, while most soldiers carried some kind of writing supplies, and, if they could find one, a deck of cards. At the start of the march, the soldiers looked adequately dressed in the sloppy manner that became a hallmark of Sherman and his army, but over time their appearance deteriorated from the wear and tear of the campaign. Numerous witnesses nonetheless observed a cockiness in their attitude. One observer stated "the whole appearance" of Sherman's soldiers was "'I can hold all the ground that I cover.'" These men were, after all, handpicked for this operation from a pool of some of the best soldiers in the war, and they knew it.

In early November 1864, Sherman issued Special Field Orders Numbers 119 and 120, outlining what he had in mind for his army. According to Illinois soldier George Cram, the general told his soldiers that they "were to prepare for a fifty-days campaign" but the soldier continued, with no sign of concern, "not a soul knows where we are going or what we are to do." Sherman told them only that he had organized them "for a special purpose" that the government and General Grant were well aware of. The Union troops were going to strike "a blow at our enemy that will have a material effect in producing what we all so much desire, his complete overthrow. . . . It is sufficient for you to know that it involves a departure from our present base, and a long and difficult march to a new one." Everything that could be thought of had been arranged, the general reported, and all Sherman asked of his men was to "maintain that discipline, patience, and courage, which have characterized you in the past." He warned them not to straggle and "be picked up by a hostile people in detail" and not to "encumber us on the march" by loading down wagons with nonessentials or encouraging "surplus servants, non-combatants, and refugees" (i.e. slaves) to tag along. "At some future time," Sherman said reflecting the Union belief that the southern elite had brought on the war, "we will be able to provide for the poor whites and blacks who seek to escape the bondage under which they are now suffering," but not now.

The most significant words of both these two orders appeared in Section 4 of Orders 120, "The army will forage liberally on the country during the march." Sherman told brigade commanders to organize foraging parties but ordered soldiers not to "enter the dwellings of the inhabitants, or commit any trespass," because corps commanders alone had "the power to destroy mills, houses, cotton-gins, etc." and then only when guerrillas "molest[ed] our march, or inhabitants . . . burn[ed] bridges, obstruct[ed] roads, or otherwise manifest[ed] local hostility." The cavalry and artillery could take horses or mules "without limit; discriminating, however, between the rich, who are usually hostile, and the poor and industrious, usually neutral or friendly." Sherman told his men to avoid "abusive or threatening language," and "endeavor to leave with each family a reasonable portion for their maintenance." Finally, corps commanders should organize "able-bodied" blacks, not into infantry units, but into pioneer battalions to keep the roads passable "so that columns will not be delayed after reaching bad places." The plan seemed so organized and reasonable.

Sherman's soldiers had such confidence in their commander that they expressed a cheerful, though careful, optimism. The Union general was a regular presence among his troops, after all, demonstrating a common touch that made the soldiers feel close to him. There was no spit and polish in William T. Sherman, as there was in many eastern generals, and he expected little in appearance from his men. The general looked for results, and his men were anxious to provide them. Sherman and his army formed a significant bond that would play a major role in the march that lay ahead.

Nowhere did this unity appear more evident than in the determination to end the war as quickly as possible. Union soldiers were ready to use destruction to achieve this end, because unlike Sherman, they detested Southerners. Sherman blamed the South for bringing on the war, but his affection for individual Southerners, gained from many years of living in the South, caused him to see destruction as the quickest way to end the war. Sherman's soldiers, however, viewed destruction as a way to punish Southerners for causing the war. So, although Sherman and his men saw the issue from different viewpoints, they were both prepared to use destructive war in their advance from Atlanta to the sea. Unlike other Union generals, Sherman would no longer try to capture and maintain command of southern terrain, but would instead destroy, and move on.

After careful preparation, Sherman had only one thing left to do before his army plunged into the Georgia countryside. The Union general decided not to leave a garrison in Atlanta because he thought it a frightful waste of Union manpower, and instead, planned to insure that Atlanta would not be militarily significant once the Union army left. Before departing the city, therefore, Sherman ordered Col. Orlando M. Poe, his talented engineering officer, to level everything of military value in the city. "Fire will do most of the work," he advised. Before Hood left Atlanta, he ordered most train equipment destroyed and exploded all the ammunition he could not carry away. Sparks from this fire had torched surrounding buildings. The famous scene of Atlanta burning in "Gone With the Wind" depicts the destruction inflicted by the retreating rebels, not the invading forces. Earlier, Confederates prepared their defenses around the city by leveling buildings to insure clear fields of fire. Departing Confederates looted on their way out of the city. Union soldier George F. Cram said that "desolation prevails. Atlanta, the beautiful, the 'Gate City' is dead." And this was the situation several weeks before Poe began his work.

Poe proceeded efficiently, destroying anything that Confederates might find helpful in continuing to wage war. Machine shops, railroad roundhouses, depots, and rolling

ORLANDO M. POE

Orlando M. Poe: Born in Navarre, Ohio, in 1832, Poe graduated from the United States Military Academy in 1856, sixth out of a class of forty-nine. When secession came, Poe was surveying the Great Lakes as a lieutenant in the topographical engineers. He soon became one of George McClellan's major subordinates. In September 1861, Poe became colonel of the 2nd Michigan Infantry Regiment, participating in McClellan's Peninsular Campaign and distinguishing himself at Williamsburg and Seven Pines. He was a brigade commander at Second Bull Run and Fredericksburg. Unfortunately the Senate failed to confirm his appointment to brigadier general of volunteers, so, for a time, he reverted to his regular army rank of captain. At Knoxville, in late 1863, he built the fortifications Ambrose Burnside used to repel James Longstreet's assaults and siege. In April 1864, Sherman named Poe chief engineer of the Military Division of the Mississippi. He served under Sherman during the Atlanta Campaign and the marches through Georgia and the Carolinas. In 1873, Poe became Sherman's personal aide in the office of commanding general and remained in that post until Sherman officially retired in 1884. Poe then continued his important engineering work on the lighthouse board, on various Great Lakes projects, and in conjunction with the building of the various transcontinental railroads. He died in 1895, from an injury suffered while inspecting canal locks on the Great Lakes. Poe, who is most famous for his systematic destruction of war material during Sherman's various campaigns in the south, was an important American military engineer in the post-war years.

stock were put to flame. A machine shop contained shells the Confederates had hidden on their departure, and its torching caused an explosion and sent sparks on to nearby buildings and set them afire. Individual Union soldiers burned vacant buildings on their own, and civilian looters joined in the activity. It looked to Union soldier William Bluffton Miller like "the destruction of Babolon," whose evil Miller likened to that of Atlanta. Like division commander William Passmore Carlin,

Miller felt sorry about what he saw, but then quickly squelched such emotion because "a Soldier is not supposed to have any conscience and must lay aside all scruples."

Despite all the destructive activity, only thirty percent of the city lay in ruins. Some four hundred buildings, mostly homes, remained undamaged when Sherman's army departed Atlanta.

3
BEGINNING THE MARCH

Reveille sounded early on the morning of November 15, 1864, the first day of the march to the sea. Soldiers had already packed what they would carry with them, placed the rest in the huts where they had been living, and then set the ramshackle structures on fire. They carried some forty days rations, and cattle ready for the slaughter followed behind. Sherman himself did not depart until the next day, nostalgically viewing the site where his friend, Maj. Gen. James B. McPherson, had died in one of the earlier battles for the city. Suffering from rheumatism in one of his arms, Sherman worried that his men expected success "as a matter of course, whereas, should we fail, this 'march' would be adjudged the wild adventure of a crazy fool."

Sherman was an impressive sight atop his horse. Tall and thin, his red hair and beard accentuating his wrinkled face and his piercing eyes, he looked very much the hard conqueror, the perpetual cigar only adding to the no-nonsense image he projected. He was lyrical as he left the city. "Behind us lay Atlanta," he later wrote, "smoldering and in ruins, the black smoke rising high in the air, and hanging like a pall over the ruined city." Ahead Sherman observed his marching troops, "Away off in the distance, on the McDonough road, was the rear of Howard's column, the gun-barrels glistening in the sun, the white-topped wagons stretching away to the south; and right before us the Fourteenth Corps, marching steadily and rapidly, with a cheery look and swinging pace, that made light of the thousand miles that lay between us and Richmond." Then, something spontaneous happened. As Sherman remembered it in his memoirs, "some band, by accident, struck up the anthem of 'John Brown's soul goes marching on'; the men caught up the strain, and never before or since have I heard the chorus of 'Glory, glory, hallelujah!' done with more spirit, or in better harmony of time and place."

The soldiers still did not know exactly where they were going. In fact, as late as December 6, as the army was nearing the coast, one soldier talked of only then learning the army's destination—and that from a Confederate newspaper he had stumbled on. Brig. Gen. William Passmore Marshall was similarly ignorant, but like the men in the ranks, he did not seem to mind. They were, after all, doing "great work that would prove decisive of the great conflict."

In reality, many soldiers had an accurate inkling of their destination. As they departed Atlanta, the troops yelled out to Sherman whenever they saw him sitting on top of his sturdy horse, "Uncle Billy, I guess Grant is waiting for us at Richmond!" The soldiers exuded confidence. One Union officer writing in his diary said, "We must succeed. Not a man in this army doubts it." Much of this confidence was the result of the soldiers' unswerving belief in Sherman's aptitude as a commander. The Union general knew what he was doing, and a vast majority of his soldiers believed they could trust their leader's ability to make this campaign a success.

Southern newspapers were not impressed. The *Richmond Examiner* called such a march a "Paradise of Fools," though the Augusta *Chronicle* advised its citizens to "pray to God, but keep your powder dry." Confederate officials, military and civil, knew that Sherman was plunging into the Georgia countryside, but could not determine his destination. Confederate leaders responded with calls to arms, beseeching Georgians to oppose the invader with everything they had. Confederate Gen. P.G.T. Beauregard, in his best bombastic style, called to the people of Georgia, "Arise to the defense of your native soil! . . . Obstruct and destroy all the roads in Sherman's front, flank, and rear, and his army will soon starve in your midst." Georgia Senator B.H. Hill was similarly forthright to his constituents, "You have now the best opportunity ever yet presented to destroy the enemy. Put everything at the disposal of our generals; remove all provisions from the path of the invader, and put all obstructions in his path." Six Georgia members of the Confederate Congress added to the hue and cry from the safety of Richmond, "Let every man fly to arms! Remove your negroes, horses, cattle, and provisions from Sherman's army, and burn what you cannot carry. Burn all bridges, and block up the roads in his route. Assail the invader in front, flank, and rear, by night and by day. Let him have no rest."

Unaware of the Confederate rhetoric, Sherman split his army into two wings after leaving Atlanta. Then they each divided in two again. The army of 62,000 traveled in a generally southeasterly direction, Slocum's wing leaving from the eastern part of Atlanta moving along the Georgia Railroad apparently toward Augusta, while Howard's wing departed from south Atlanta and moved along the Macon & Western Railroad toward Macon. In reality, the two wings were heading for neither city; their goal was actually the Georgia state capital of Milledgeville. Sherman successfully fooled the Confederates into defending Augusta, Macon, Millen, Savannah, and Charleston. The four corps traveled on four roughly parallel

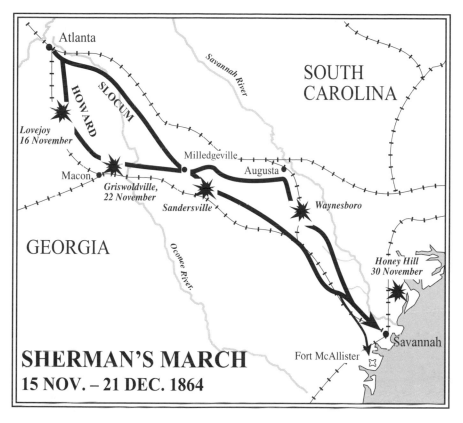

Atlanta

SOUTH CAROLINA

Savannah River

HOWARD

SLOCUM

Lovejoy
16 November

Milledgeville

Augusta

Macon

Griswoldville,
22 November

Sandersville

Waynesboro

GEORGIA

Oconee River

Honey Hill
30 November

Savannah

SHERMAN'S MARCH

Fort McAllister

15 NOV. – 21 DEC. 1864

roads, five to fifteen miles apart, with Kilpatrick's Third Cavalry Division protecting the flanks and rear. The column varied in width, sometimes spreading out over sixty miles. Sherman knew the geography of the area well, both from his pre-war travel and residence and from his recent study of maps and the latest census. The Union general's leadership remained steady and sure. Messengers constantly galloped between the columns, and sometimes signal rockets lit up the night skies.

The make-up of the corps columns was unlike that of any other fighting unit. At the head might be cavalry or black pioneers, followed by a regiment of troops which took care of any enemy resistance. Then came the mass of infantry, walking

JOSEPH E. BROWN

Joseph E. Brown: Born in Pickens District, South Carolina, in 1820, Brown moved to Georgia with his family in 1830, and gained an admiration for the no-nonsense leadership of Andrew Jackson and the states rights ideas of John C. Calhoun. During the 1840s as a young man, Brown attended school in South Carolina. He went on to teach school in Georgia, and was admitted to the Georgia bar in 1845. The following year, Brown graduated from Yale Law School and began his practice in Canton, Georgia. He won a seat in the Georgia legislature as a Jacksonian in 1849, but served only one term. In 1855, Brown was appointed a superior court judge, resigning in 1857 to campaign for and win election to the office of governor. He was reelected three times and resigned in 1865 when the Confederacy collapsed. Brown was a committed slave owner and extreme states righter, and these allowed him to provide effective leadership for Georgia's departure from the Union. Even before Georgia's secession, he had the state militia capture Fort Pulaski, and he energetically recruited soldiers for the cause. Quickly, however, the Georgia governor became a problem for the Confederate war effort. He retained his states rights beliefs and insisted that Jefferson Davis's policies were impinging on them. Brown spoke out vociferously against any policies or laws coming out of the Confederate capital that he feared would undermine the rights of the individual states. He and Jefferson Davis conducted a regular and usually acerbic correspondence over such issues as conscription, national taxes, *habeas corpus*, and the use of Georgia troops in areas far from home. Brown, along with other Georgia leaders, fled Milledgeville at the approach of Sherman, and was briefly imprisoned in Washington at war's end. After his imprisonment, Brown shocked Georgians by calling for cooperation with Reconstruction and by becoming a Republican. He was chief justice of the Georgia Supreme Court from 1868 to 1870, and then returned to the Democratic Party in 1871, supporting Horace Greeley for the presidency. Brown became wealthy through his presidency of the Western and Atlantic Railroad Company and his real estate activity in Atlanta. He served in the United States Senate from 1880 to 1891 and later became a leading figure in the state's Populist party. He died in Atlanta in 1894. During the Civil War, his repeated refusal to cooperate with the Confederate national government exasperated Jefferson Davis and hindered the southern war effort.

four abreast, with supply wagons directly behind each brigade. Finally, pontoon wagons rumbled along, followed by herds of cattle, and the rear guard. Cavalry or infantry protected the flanks, and units rotated their position in the column every day. To Georgians it was an amazing sight, frightening to the core. A teenage girl wrote, "it seemed . . . the whole world was coming." An aged black man marveled that "Dar's millions of 'em, millions! . . . Is there anybody lef' up North?"

The state into which the army plunged was a big place. It comprised more area (60,000 square miles) than any other state east of the Mississippi River, and its one million residents, of whom almost forty-five percent were slaves, made it the third most populous state in the Confederacy. Its fourth term governor, Joseph E. Brown, had conducted a running feud with Confederate President Jefferson Davis over state versus national power, but his popularity remained high in the state, gaining re-election in 1863 by a large margin. William J. Hardee, a native Georgian, served as commander of the Department of South Carolina, Georgia and Florida, and the state had a great deal of confidence in him. Similarly popular was Jefferson Davis's appointment of P.G.T. Beauregard to the new Military Division of the West, placing Beauregard in charge of Hood in Tennessee and Richard Taylor in Mississippi. Joseph Wheeler commanded the cavalry, while Gustavus W. Smith commanded the meager Georgia Militia. In all, these separated troops, not counting Hood, numbered around 30,000 men, more than enough, if massed, to create disaster for the invading Federals. Another thirty regiments of Georgia soldiers were fighting with Lee in Virginia and not available for defense of their homeland.

Georgia's landscape is a mixture of red clay hills and sandy level terrain. Near the coast the terrain turns marshy. In 1864, Georgia consisted of a region of some large plantations and many small self-reliant farms of two hundred acres or so, raising crops and livestock. The state contained twice as many

This photograph illustrates how Union forces destroyed railroad lines.

pigs and horses as people; and corn predominated among the grains, although vegetables, like sweet potatoes, were also plentiful. Cotton was the cash crop, and some of the land owners had become prosperous thanks to slave labor. Near the coast, rice and sugar cane could be found. As more than one observer noted, Georgia was "the breadbasket of the Confederacy." The towns were small county seats, but some, like Madison, had impressive columned homes.

The typical farm was equally divided into cleared land and woods, with a house, barn, slave quarters, and various other outbuildings. Farm houses stood about half a mile apart along rough roads, and these buildings generally consisted of logs. One of Sherman's officers said that "at a distance, the master's mansion sometimes is hardly distinguishable from the cottages of the slaves." Georgia was hardly a region covered with white pillared plantation houses. The state's wealth was less conspicuous but real nonetheless. Georgia provided food for the Confederate army, and would soon feed the invading Federals.

HENRY W. SLOCUM

Henry W. Slocum: Born in Onondaga County, New York, in 1827, Slocum graduated from the United States Military Academy in 1857, where he was a roommate of Philip Sheridan. After four years of routine duty in the artillery, Slocum resigned his commission to become a lawyer in Syracuse. When secession came, he became colonel of the 27th Infantry Regiment which took heavy casualties at First Bull Run, Slocum himself being wounded in the thigh. He gained brigade and then division command and participated in all the major eastern battles until sent to Chattanooga with Hooker. Refusing to serve under Hooker because he considered him incompetent, Slocum remained in rear areas until Hooker's 1864 resignation brought him back as a corps commander in the latter stages of the battles around Atlanta. Upon that city's capture, Slocum served as its military governor. Sherman named him commander of his left wing during the marches to the sea and through the Carolinas. Once the war was over, Slocum resigned his commission and became a Democratic Party activist, serving three terms in Congress from a Brooklyn district (1869-1873, 1883-1885). He was also a member of the Gettysburg Monument Commission. He died in Brooklyn and is buried there. A favorite of Sherman's, Slocum's feud with Hooker and his conversion to the Democratic Party prevented him from gaining the military and civilian success that might otherwise have been his.

As Sherman stated prior to his departure from Atlanta, "Where a million people live, I have no fear of getting a share."

The first day out of Atlanta, cold rain began to fall and continued for the next week, making the roads muddy and the men miserable but optimistic nonetheless. Sherman traveled with the XIV Corps of Slocum's left wing, Slocum later remembering that his commander was characteristically gregarious about all matters but the march itself. Sherman asked no advice or gave no intimation of his hopes and plans. That night the army camped near Livonia, with Stone Mountain clearly visible ahead. The men destroyed railroad tracks, using tools Colonel

Poe provided for twisting the iron rails to prevent their re-use. Sherman took an active interest in the work, telling the men that, while the tools worked well, he preferred starting a bonfire of railroad ties, placing the rails across the fire until the middles became red hot, and then twisting them around a telegraph pole or nearby tree. The result of such effort gained the name "Sherman's neckties" or "Sherman's hairpins," although some of the soldiers grew ingenious enough to twist rails into the letters "U.S." and then to leave them in conspicuous places as markers of their passage.

Sherman moved constantly as the four columns advanced, and his men saw him frequently and cheered and yelled "Uncle Billy, Uncle Billy," when he came into view. He acknowledged the cheers and absentmindedly looked around to see his location and identify where he would ride next. Usually Sherman traveled through the fields and refused to break into a marching unit, waiting until it had passed by and then falling in behind. He insisted that the soldiers had the right of way.

On November 17, Sherman and the XIV Corps approached the town of Covington and demonstrated their confidence by holding a parade through the town. Bands played, color bearers displayed their flags, and the soldiers fell into step. Townspeople, both black and white, came out to watch in awe at the panoply before them. The slaves were particularly excited, joyfully jumping up and down at the appearance of the soldiers. Sherman became a center of attraction, the conqueror on his horse. So many people wanted to see and touch him that he took a side street away from the main column to escape the on-rush of humanity. Union troops now became the beneficiaries of the excitement. At the request of the mayor, several officers enjoyed a turkey dinner initially meant for Sherman.

Four miles out of town, Sherman stopped the column for the night. Ever curious, he took to walking the nearby countryside. Sherman arrived at a farm house to find the whites gone but the blacks, including an old man with an impressive head of gray hair, watching the proceedings. The general began conversing with the man, trying to see if the former slaves understood what was going on. The old man responded affirmatively; he waited for the "angel of the Lord" to come and free him, and that day had now arrived. The former slave realized that Federal leaders insisted the army fought for the preservation of the Union, but most slaves, the old man stated, knew the real cause of the war and a Federal victory would result in freedom.

Sherman agreed that the coming of the army meant freedom, but he told the man that the slaves, so freed, should stay put and not follow the columns. The Union army could not feed both freed slaves and soldiers. Extra people, Sherman explained, would only hinder the army's progress. The Union general stated that a few young men might come along as pioneers, but other former slaves should not follow the army. Sherman understood that the Union advance brought freedom to black people, but he did not want civilians following the army columns. Like the press and humanitarian agents, Sherman considered extra followers an encumbrance, who had to be kept away.

Sherman quickly learned that his foraging orders were interpreted loosely. On this same plantation, he saw one soldier walking along a road loaded down with ham, sorghummolasses, and honey. Seeing Sherman, the soldier remarked in a stage whisper, clearly audible to those nearby, "Forage liberally on the country," quoting the phrase from Sherman's order. The general looked the private in the eye and told him that taking liberally from all farms was not what the order meant; only properly constituted patrols were to forage, and anything so gathered was to be turned over to commissary officers for sharing with the entire column. Significantly, however, Sherman made no effort to confiscate the goods from the man, and word must have spread quickly throughout the army that

A sketch depicting Union soldiers foraging "liberally" on the Georgia countryside.

the commanding general was accepting the broadest interpretation of his order. Such was indeed the case. Sherman's application of destructive and psychological warfare would benefit from random acts of individuals as much as from the organized foraging parties. Sherman realized that if soldiers were hungry, they could not carry out the destructive war he had planned.

4

MILLEDGEVILLE, THE CAPTURE OF GEORGIA'S CAPITAL

Sherman's army pressed forward to little opposition. Slocum continued to try and make the Confederates believe his wing was headed towards Augusta while it was actually turning towards Milledgeville. At the same time, Howard's right wing proceeded along two roads, paralleling the Macon & Western Railroad, and seemingly still moving in the direction of Macon. The troops continued their systematic wreckage of the railroad and filled their wagons and knapsacks with the region's produce. Elements of Maj. Gen. Joseph Wheeler's 3,500 cavalry had tried to slow down the Union advance from the start, at East Point, Rough and Ready, Jonesboro, Stockbridge, and Lovejoy's Station. Each time, however, a unit of Kilpatrick's 5,000 horsemen brushed the Confederates aside.

As the Union horsemen made their feint at Macon, Wheeler tried to block them again with 2,000 of his men, digging in

JOSEPH WHEELER

Joseph Wheeler: Born in Augusta, Georgia, in 1836, Wheeler lived in Connecticut as a child before his father brought the family back to Georgia in 1845. In 1859 he graduated nineteenth in a class of twenty-two at the United States Military Academy. After brief service in

the Mounted Rifles of the United Sates Army, Wheeler resigned his commission when secession came and joined the Confederate cause. He was a regimental commander at Shiloh and Perryville; and in July 1862, Braxton Bragg appointed him chief of cavalry of the Army of Mississippi. Wheeler and Nathan Bedford Forrest both served under Bragg but could not get along, so Forrest was reassigned elsewhere and Wheeler became commander of cavalry in the Army of Tennessee. Wheeler held that position at Chattanooga and during the Atlanta campaign. When Hood took the Army of Tennessee north, Wheeler and his cavalry corps remained behind to try to contain Sherman. He had little success during the marches to the sea and through the Carolinas. In fact, the pillaging and destruction his troops practiced on the people of Georgia aided Sherman's implementation of psychological warfare. During the march through the Carolinas, Wade Hampton replaced Wheeler as overall cavalry commander, and once again Wheeler's horsemen had few successes and continued to inflict havoc on civilians. Wheeler was captured at war's end and spent a month in prison at Fort Delaware. For four years, he was a New Orleans entrepreneur, moving to Alabama in 1869 to become a planter and a lawyer. Wheeler was a Democratic congressman from Alabama (1881 to 1883, 1885 to 1899), and was a major general of volunteers during the Spanish-American War. He died in Brooklyn in 1906. Because of his Spanish-American War service, Wheeler is one of only a few Confederates buried in the Arlington National Cemetery. Wheeler participated in more than one hundred Civil war battles or skirmishes, was wounded three times, had thirty-six staff officers shot at his side, and sixteen horses shot out from under him, which gained him the nickname "Fighting Joe." The story is told that, during a Spanish-American War battle, he forgot where he was and yelled at his troops to attack those "Yankees."

some four miles outside the city. Kilpatrick attacked vigorously and drove the Confederates back. He then continued efforts to convince the Confederates that the rest of the Union army would soon be attacking Macon.

Wheeler took the ruse as did Gov. Joe Brown, leading politician Robert Toombs, and Generals William Hardee, Richard Taylor, Howell Cobb, and P.G.T. Beauregard, all of whom were in Macon, or on the way to an emergency summit meeting there. Sherman thoroughly confused the Confederates when the expected attack on the city never materialized. Hardee left for the Atlantic coast, but he first ordered Gen. Gustavus W. Smith and his pitiful force of 3,000 Georgia militia to move toward Augusta, where Sherman was next expected to surface.

At this point, on November 21, the only major skirmish of the march took place. The Georgia militia, under the temporary command of an inexperienced general named Pleasant J. Phillips, had moved to protect Augusta and its munitions factories which Georgia leaders assumed Sherman intended to target. Sherman did not plan to attack the munitions factories, but his feint in that direction brought part of the Union army to Griswoldville. Near that village, the Georgia militia ran into a brigade of Federals acting as a rear guard for Osterhaus's XV Corps of Howard's wing. The Confederates' orders were to avoid any conflict this side of Augusta, but Phillips, seeing that his 3,000 men outnumbered Brig. Gen. Charles C. Walcutt's 1,500 man brigade, foolishly decided to attack. Phillips ignored the fact that the veteran Federals had thrown up temporary entrenchments, and the Confederate general did not realize that one of Walcutt's regiments was armed with Spencer repeating rifles.

Behind their entrenchments on a small hill, the Federals were preparing a meal when Phillips deployed his men into three battle lines in an open field before the Union soldiers. Walcutt quickly ordered his men to the entrenchments, but told

PETER J. OSTERHAUS

Peter J. Osterhaus: Born in Coblenz, Prussia, in 1823, Osterhaus was a refugee to the United States from Europe's Revolutions of 1848, settling in the large German community in St. Louis. A military school graduate and member of the Prussian army, Osterhaus entered the American Civil War as major of "Osterhaus's Missouri Battalion." Rising to regimental command, he fought in the major Missouri battles of 1861 and 1862. He served under Sherman during the Vicksburg Campaign and was wounded at the Big Black River but missed only two days of service. Osterhaus fought well during the Union army's charge up Missionary Ridge at Chattanooga. Despite Sherman's anger at his political activities, Osterhaus became major general in July 1864 during the Atlanta Campaign. He was corps commander during the march to the sea and the early part of the Carolinas march, and then became chief of staff to Edward Canby during the Mobile campaign. Osterhaus left the military in 1866 and served as United States consul in France (1866-1877) and deputy consul in Germany (1898-1900). He also ran a wholesale hardware business during the post-war years. In 1916, while the United States prepared to enter World War I, he was living in Duisburg, Germany, on a Civil War veteran's pension. He died before American troops arrived. Osterhaus was one of the best military leaders of the many foreign born Americans who served on the Union side in the Civil War.

them to hold their fire until the Confederates were practically in the Union defenses. Federal volleys then tore giant holes in the Confederate attack lines, the Spencer rifles delivering a particularly devastating storm of lead. The Confederates fell in large numbers, but survivors kept attacking until they could not take it anymore and broke for the cover of a nearby ravine. This short battle proved a disaster for the Georgia militia which suffered fifty-one killed and 472 wounded, compared to only thirteen dead and seventy-nine wounded for the Federals.

Union Brig. Gen. Charles C. Walcutt.

It was, as one Union participant described it, "A harvest of death." In the aftermath, Union soldiers searched the area before their lines and found, to their dismay, that the attacking Confederates had included old men and young boys. In one instance, troops discovered a wounded teenage boy lying next to his dead father, two brothers, and an uncle. As they spent the night trying to help the wounded, the Federals asked themselves: what kind of army would throw such people into the fight?

Griswoldville proved to be the sole example of set combat during the march. Sherman had maneuvered his forces so effectively (with Hood's inept help), that no significant opposition existed before the Union army. While implementing a modern war of destruction against southern society, Sherman also achieved the major principle of traditional nineteenth century warfare: he had positioned Union forces so that they were able to move against fractions of the enemy. Beyond this, however, they could live off the land and destroy at will. In brief, Sherman had militarily and psychologically outflanked his Confederate opposition.

Sherman's decision to bypass Augusta and its munitions factories confused his opponents. To the present day, there is a story told that Sherman did not occupy and destroy Augusta because a former girlfriend lived there. Another tale talks of his first-born son having been buried in Augusta

HOWELL COBB

Howell Cobb: Born in Jefferson County, Georgia, in 1815, Cobb was an 1834 graduate of Franklin College (later University of Georgia), and became a lawyer in Athens in 1836. For the next four years he was also solicitor general for a judicial district within the state. He was a member of the United States House of Representatives from 1843 to 1851, first as a Democrat and then as a Whig. Cobb was Speaker of the House from 1849 to 1851. He returned to Georgia to serve as its governor from 1851 to 1853, at that time a firm unionist. From 1855 to 1857 Cobb served as Chairman of the Ways and Means Committee, and from 1857 to 1860 he was secretary of the treasury in the James Buchanan administration. Cobb supported secession, and when it came, was one of the several individuals mentioned for the presidency of the Confederacy. He presided over the Montgomery convention and then was president of the Provisional Confederate Congress. Cobb joined the Confederate Army in July 1861 as colonel of the 16th Georgia Infantry Regiment and rose to the ranks of major general by September 1863. He fought at Seven Pines, the Seven Days, Second Bull Run, and Antietam among other battles, and, in 1863, he served on a court of inquiry investigating the Confederate losses at Vicksburg, Jackson, and Port Hudson. Named commander of the District of Georgia in 1863, Cobb acted as a referee between President Jefferson Davis and Gov. Joseph E. Brown. He defeated Union Gen. George Stoneman at Macon in 1864, but Cobb played only a minor role in the unsuccessful attempt to combat Sherman's marches across Georgia and through the Carolinas. Cobb surrendered at Macon, and in the post-war years had a law practice there, but held no political office. In 1868, he died during a trip to New York City and is buried in Athens, Georgia. Cobb's major contribution to the Confederate war effort was political more than military, for example, his particularly successful attempt to moderate the dispute between the Confederate president and the Georgia governor.

when Sherman had been stationed there in 1844. Both stories have no basis in fact. Sherman did not marry until 1850, and there is no evidence he had a girlfriend there. Despite that, such tales about Sherman's march, most of them of a harsher variety, abound. In truth, Sherman bypassed Augusta because he did not want to fight a battle there. Because Union troops were living off the land, the general could not risk running out of food by stopping to assail a town. During the post-war era, when Sherman was asked about marching by Augusta, he said archly that, if citizens there felt snubbed, he would be happy to organize some of his old soldiers and do the job then.

Union troops marched onward, Sherman riding with the XIV Corps of Slocum's left wing. On November 22, the weather remained cold and wet enough for Sherman to fortify himself against the piercing fall wind with a drink and his usual cigar. The columns were now some ten miles shy of Milledgeville. Sherman found a log house that would provide him shelter for the night. As he looked around one of the rooms, he found a small box with the name "Howell Cobb" written on it. A slave then verified what this box indicated: Sherman was on the plantation of the former Speaker of the U.S. House of Representatives and cabinet member and presently a Confederate general, one of the individuals at the Confederate summit in Macon. Sherman was determined to make Cobb pay for his role in secession. He told his soldiers to strip the place completely. The large plantation was rich in vegetables and produce of all kinds, so Union soldiers filled their sacks. That night they warded off the cold with bonfires fed by the plantation's fence rails.

As Sherman sat in his chair, his rain-soaked back to a warming fire place, he became aware that someone was watching him, an old slave carrying a candle in his hand. "What do you want, old man?" Sherman asked. The black man responded: "Dey say you is Massa Sherman." That was correct, Sherman answered, what did he want? The black man, over-awed, could only keep repeating: "Dis nigger can't sleep dis night." The old man worried about committing himself further until he knew for certain that he was speaking to Union soldiers, and not Confederate imposters. Recently, some of Wheeler's cavalrymen had pretended to be Federals and had severely beaten the slaves for being friendly to the enemy. Sherman told the man to go outdoors and look at the bonfires alight as far as the eye could see on all horizons. Had the old man ever seen anything like that before, Sherman asked? No, the man admitted, as he realized his dream had finally come true. The Federal army and freedom were in Georgia at last.

In Milledgeville, the broad boulevarded capital of Georgia, the members of the legislature were in a panic over the approach of the Union army. Giving in to Gov. Joe Brown's impassioned plea of November 19, 1864, the legislature voted, on November 22, to institute a draft of all Georgian males between sixteen and sixty-five years of age. Brown, meanwhile, pardoned 175 of the 200 convicts in the state penitentiary, those willing to join the army. (And, apparently, they promptly set fire to the prison.) In all, there were fewer than 700 Confederate troops available in the town of 2,300 people— young boys, old men, and the recently released prisoners. This tiny ill-prepared force stood no chance against Sherman's army. The state legislature decided to get out of town immediately. Governor Brown, newly returned from Macon, began frantically loading furniture and other material on the last train leaving the city, stripping the governor's mansion, taking even vegetables from the kitchen. The legislators were just as quick to flee, many, like Brown, escaping to Macon.

Unlike the state leaders, most of Milledgeville's citizens decided to remain. For a day, there was civilian plundering, but when the first Union troops arrived on the afternoon of November 22, the army put a stop to the looting. The 107th New York Regiment, XX Corps, Slocum's wing, raised the American flag over the capitol. That same day, Jefferson Davis entreated Georgia officials, now scattered to the wind, to burn bridges, topple trees, bury torpedoes in the road, and do whatever necessary to "obstruct the advance of the enemy."

Sherman and his staff did not reach Milledgeville until the following morning, November 23, 1864. The commanding general quickly learned that the entire left wing was encircling the city, while Howard's right wing was in its proper position around Gordon, some twelve miles away. As Sherman subsequently phrased it in his memoirs: "The first stage of the journey was, therefore, complete, and absolutely successful." The army had traveled one hundred miles since leaving Atlanta, destroyed many miles of railroad and military and civilian property, stripped the countryside of produce and forage, and brought terror to the civilian population.

Sherman saw that the governor and legislature had abandoned the city and its inhabitants to the Union army and that the people of Milledgeville were not happy about the frantic departure of their state officials. Disgusted citizens told Sherman about the governor filling a train of freight cars with furnishings from the governor's mansion. They were particularly upset about the vegetables he took from the kitchen and cellar, while leaving behind weaponry and state records. Sherman spent the night in the empty mansion, sleeping on the bare floor. He read newspapers for the first time since his departure from Atlanta and found humor in the Confederate calls for the destruction and burning of everything in his path, prohibiting the Union army's survival off the land. The general considered such appeals to be empty rhetoric. He had seen himself that Georgia citizens were not taking orders from their leaders but instead were growing angry at their directives. Sherman's psychological warfare was beginning to take its toll. The further Sherman marched, the wider southern fear became. All over the South, people worried that Sherman was on his way to their locale. But this anxiety was misplaced. Sherman could not be in one part of Georgia and everywhere else too. Still, such dread served his purposes well.

The army gorged itself on the bountiful supply of food it found in the Milledgeville area, celebrating Thanksgiving day, a holiday that Abraham Lincoln had established only the previous year. Finding the state capitol vacant, some of Sherman's soldiers decided to enjoy a farce. In what one Indiana soldier called "regular southern fire eating style," they voted themselves the Georgia legislature, elected a speaker, and passed a resolution repealing the state's secession ordinance. When someone shouted: "The Yankees are coming." the pretend legislators mocked the actions of the real law makers by running out in panic. Later, another group of soldiers held a mock funeral for Gov. Joe Brown.

While this satire was harmless, other soldiers roamed the statehouse building filling their pockets full of newly printed Confederate money and wantonly tossing library books and government documents out the windows. At the arsenal, soldiers found two to three thousand pikes, some shotguns and old muskets, and, a Union officer reported in his diary, "about 10,000 large butcher knives the blade of which was about 18 to 20 inches long." When the officer asked the slaves about these knives, they responded that their purpose was "to cut Yankee hearts out." "It is one of old Joe Browns ideas," the Union officer surmised, "and like him has vanished." Sherman's men enjoyed brandishing these weapons while pretending they were Georgia legislators.

Except for this rowdiness at the capitol, the soldiers did little damage to non-military buildings or material in the city. On Sherman's orders, they destroyed the arsenal and several public buildings that might be of use to the Confederate military, but they generally left private property alone. The governor's mansion was ransacked of furniture, not by the Federals, but by local citizens.

During the army's sumptuous thanksgiving dinner, several prisoners of war, escapees from Andersonville, some one hundred miles away, came staggering into the city. They were emaciated and hungry, driven to tears at the sight of the American flag and the smell of food. Those soldiers who saw

ALPHEUS S. WILLIAMS

Alpheus S. Williams: Born in Saybrook, Connecticut, in 1810, Williams graduated from Yale University in 1831. After three years of law studies and travel abroad, Williams began a law practice in Detroit in 1836. During the 1840s he held office as probate judge and city postmaster, owned a newspaper, and served in the Mexican War. When secession came, Williams helped organize Michigan's preparation for war. In August 1861 he gained the rank of brigadier general and fought in the Shenandoah Valley in 1862. He served in all the important battles in the East, rising to acting corps commander in the Army of the Potomac. After Gettysburg, Williams held both division and corps commands in the Army of the Cumberland, serving under Sherman during the Atlanta campaign and the marches to the sea and through the Carolinas. He remained in the army until January 1866 and then served for three years as United States minister to El Salvador. In 1870, Williams failed in his run as a Democrat for the governorship of Michigan. He did win election, however, to two terms in Congress (1875-1879) but died during his second term. Williams is buried in Detroit. The oldest of Sherman's corps commander, his nickname was "Old Pap."

them became angered at the sight, and they wondered how Confederates could treat enemy soldiers in such a brutal way. Sherman's soldiers grew even more determined to punish the South. Yet, because it was out of the line of his march, Sherman made no attempt to liberate the sufferers in the prison. The general's goal was to end the war as quickly as possible, thus liberating all prisoners.

On November 24, Sherman, now accompanying Williams' XX Corps, moved out of Milledgeville with Slocum's left wing. At the same time, Howard's right wing left Gordon, the four corps columns remaining in roughly parallel formation. They were a week into the march and, despite the bad weather, they were making good progress, about a third of the way toward their goal of reaching the sea. Fortunately for the traveling army, the weather began to clear up. The rain ceased, it grew warmer, and the muddy road began to turn hard again.

5

MARCHING, FORAGING, AND DESTROYING

Life in the army settled into a regular rhythm. The men became used to marching in the four corps column formation, with the cavalry darting in and out. Reveille, sounded by shrill bugles and beating drums, awakened the sleeping men at day break or earlier every day. Almost instantly, the tent cities thrown up the night before grew noisy with the movement of 62,000 men, spread out over twenty to sixty miles. Soldiers cooked their breakfasts, eating well if foragers the day before had been successful, or subsisting on hardtack and army bacon if not. The encampments were quickly dismembered, and, at the sound of more bugles and drums, the men formed their columns for the day's march.

Sherman's plan called for the army to move fifteen miles each day, an ambitious goal that was often reached. By now the men in the marching columns had learned to destroy railroads with an amazing efficiency. A regiment would form a line on one side of the tracks and, on order, turn the ties and rails over. The rails were then heated on a bonfire of the ties and twisted beyond further use. Also destroyed was anything associated with slavery, prisoners of war, or the Confederate war effort in general. For example, the soldiers routinely killed dogs of any size or age because slaves and escaped prisoners of war had repeatedly told them how the Confederates used dogs to track down escapees and fugitives.

Black workers, both soldiers and run-away slaves, ensured passable roads, clearing obstructions of natural and Confederate variety, and making log corduroy pathways where necessary. When conditions were particularly bad, Union troops pitched in, the officers included. It was not unusual to see a general, even Sherman, putting his shoulder into some task. Rivers and creeks too deep to cross without aid were traversed by pontoon bridges with planking extending to both banks.

The men marched all day, usually not stopping for lunch. They ate when and however they could, Sherman insisting that the columns inexorably press forward. They normally marched for fifty minutes and rested for ten. There were also irregular rest breaks, and at that time the men might catch a few extra winks of sleep, play cards, write in a diary, smoke a pipe, or trade jokes and songs. As they marched, the soldiers were a noisy bunch. Having no fear of attack, their march discipline was loose. The columns stopped for the night, depending on the distance covered and their arrival at a suitable camp site. The availability of water was a particularly important consideration.

When a campsite was reached, each man connected his tent half with another man's, pitched the tent, started cooking fires, and consumed the only full meal of the day. As night fell, the sea of campfires created a spectacular scene commented on by Sherman and by the commonest soldier alike. The men ate their dinners in leisure and gathered close around the campfire to enjoy each other's company and take care of such necessary chores as tending to the variety of pets that many of them carried along. Cock fighting was a popular sport of this predominantly rural soldiery. They also enjoyed telling war stories, sharing their adventures of the day.

One center of attention was the foragers, whose return in the afternoon or early evening was occasion for great anticipation and hubbub. The marching soldiers were particularly interested in what the men had seen and done in their movement on the flanks and in front of the columns and whether or not the foragers had skirmished against Wheeler's cavalry. Even more importantly, the troops were concerned with what provisions the foraging parties had found. Sometimes when a unit's foragers did not make it back on time, their absence meant little or nothing to eat at supper or breakfast. Or, a forager might be killed in the midst of his search, leaving a number of soldiers hungry. During the march, Joe Wheeler's Confederate cavalry slit the throats, hanged, or shot some sixty of Sherman's men. Numerous soldiers told of coming upon foragers who had been hanged, or executed, with knife or by gun shot, at close range. Sometimes these gruesome sights bore a hand-lettered sign reading: "Death to all Foragers."

According to Sherman's order at the beginning of the march, foraging parties were to be organized and travel the countryside under the direction of an officer. But, as Sherman's own early run-in with an independent forager showed, this system quickly broke down. Units still sent men out to gather food for the army, but control over them was slight, at best. Once foragers fanned out in all directions from the marching columns, they broke into small groups, sometimes one or two alone, and they ran their own operations. All that officers demanded of them was to return on time in the evening and share their booty with the men in the ranks.

Stories abound about the return of the foragers, their accomplishments the source of vivid narrative. One midnight, after being gone for several days, a man named Snipe and several fellow foragers roused the regiment from its sleep. Snipe had six mules and horses "strung together with a motley assortment of improvised harness, made up of all sorts of odds and ends of leather, rope and iron chain. . . . His wagon was an immense box of the Tennessee pattern . . . filled to the guards with the choicest of wines and liquors" which he soon shared with his own regiment and others on either side of it.

Men like Snipe quickly gained the name "bummer." Before the march, this term referred to a soldier who, like those portrayed in later motion picture and television war films, barely tolerated discipline and normally did whatever he could get away with. Yet, when crisis came, he was an excellent soldier. In Sherman's army, a bummer, at first, was a soldier who took on foraging without officer authorization. Quickly, however, Sherman's troops began calling anyone who regularly foraged a bummer. One of Sherman's officers left this colorful description: "Fancy a ragged man, blackened by the smoke of many a pine knot fire, mounted on a scrawny mule, without a saddle, with a gun, a knapsack, a butcher knife and a plug hat, stealing his way through the pine forests far out on the flanks of a column. Keen on the scent of rebels, or bacon, or silver spoons, or corn, or anything valuable, and you have him in your mind."

This forager, or bummer, left the main column early in the morning, either walking or riding some kind of horse or mule earlier taken from a Georgia farm. He would usually travel about five miles from the column, though at times he might double that distance. As quickly as he could, the bummer attempted to find a wagon of some kind and a pack animal to pull it, the most convenient way to get his booty back to his unit. He might not always be so lucky and would then have to load down his own horse or mule and literally cover his body with his treasure.

A sketch portraying a typical "bummer."

The bummer's days were rarely dull, sometimes dangerous, and usually successful. He and his colleagues became highly skilled at ferreting out plant and animal food, and discovering where Southerners had hidden the family silverware or other valuables. Even when whites stayed with their homes and property, and most did not, the bummers, expert interrogators, often tricked the information out of their victims. Slaves left behind with the property were another sure source of information to the foraging parties. Often angry at their master or mistress for possible mistreatment or for being left behind, slaves might tell all with little coaxing, or they might accidentally give out such information, or the bummers might have to threaten it out of them. Whatever the case, the bummers, more often than not, found supplies on the farms and plantations they visited.

Reflecting nineteenth century American racism, bummers viewed the slaves negatively and were not above taking advantage of them, even in their modest circumstances. Slave cabins often received thorough pillaging. In most cases, however, whether dealing with blacks or whites, the bummers did not inflict physical harm on their victims. They might even be courteous, or at other times physically threatening, but normally they did not kill or maim the victims of their pillaging.

They were particularly solicitous of white women, once again reflecting nineteenth century views. Rape of white women was rare. The number of black women violated is uncertain, but it was no doubt more extensive. According to historian Joseph Glatthaar, health statistics indicate that sexual promiscuity was uncommon. He found that, from November 1864 to April 1865, the time when Sherman was marching through Georgia and the Carolinas, his soldiers averaged fifteen cases of venereal disease per 10,000 soldiers. The Union army elsewhere averaged sixty cases per 10,000, or four times the rate in Sherman's army. The Confederate venereal disease rate is unknown.

The fact that many Georgia men were willing to run away and leave their families in Sherman's path, and the frequent hiding of valuables in women's clothes indicates that southern whites did not worry excessively about physical violence against their female family members. It is also significant that southern and northern soldiers did not write about sexual crimes even though sex was a matter of great curiosity and interest to fighting men on both sides. The incidence of illicit sex with white or black women during the march to the sea, therefore, seems to have been slight, despite the myths that later grew up about the subject.

Bummers frequently showed concern about families on farms they visited and had an especial interest in any baby they might see. Writing after the war, a white Southerner said she heard many stores like the one about a Union soldier, who, while guarding a house, became concerned about a crying baby. The mother told him that the baby cried from hunger. The soldier became teary-eyed and provided her with whatever food he could find. Another soldier wrote to his father about his readiness to burn down a house when a ten-year-old girl asked him not to. She had "such a pleading look," he said, "that I could not have the heart to fire the place." The bummers came and took what they wanted, but they often did so in the most curiously courteous manner possible. They sometimes left enough provisions to feed a family they could have stripped of all food.

Other bummers were nasty and threatening, however, promising the most dire consequences to those who refused to cooperate. When they found a vacated farm, they plundered indiscriminately and might very well burn outbuildings or the main house itself, something they normally avoided if the structures were occupied. Even Unionists were not safe. An Indiana soldier said that if individuals were loyal, "they can afford to contribute something to help us carry on the war and if they are Rebels we will take it anyway."

Sherman's army thus inflicted a huge amount of damage, yet it did not pursue a scorched earth policy. As historian Mark Grimsley and others have demonstrated, Sherman's destruction was done with a purpose and was not indiscriminately brutal. In the mid 1950s a University of Georgia geographer, D.J. DeLaubenfels, did a careful study of the buildings in a sixty mile area from Covington to Milledgeville. He found that of the seventy-two houses standing in the region before the visit of Sherman's army, some twenty-two were still standing in 1955 and nine others had been demolished after the Civil War. Thirty-one houses in one part of the path of Sherman's army, therefore, were certifiably not destroyed by the Union army. Another twenty-seven discoverable sites provided no information on the disposition of the houses there, while eleven building sites could not be found. In conclusion, DeLaubenfels said that "a great many houses, perhaps even most of them, escaped destruction during the march to the sea."

Stories are legion of southern white women standing up to the Union invaders, an occurrence which sometimes happened. An Indiana soldier told of a Georgia white woman spitting in a soldier's face while calling him a variety of names. Another soldier remembered a woman with children at her side promising with great vehemence: "Our men will fight you as long as they live, and these boys'll fight you when they grow up." Historian Jacqueline Glass Campbell argues in her study of Sherman's later march through the Carolinas in early 1865, that southern white women shocked Sherman's soldiers with the fierceness of their opposition and, rather than becoming demoralized, they became more resolute in their support of the Confederate cause. Lisa Tendrich Frank makes the same point about women during the march to the sea. Such bravado occurred, of course, and post-war female animosity is well known, but it was not nearly as universal as often portrayed in post-war writings. The approach of Sherman's army frightened southern white women, who had heard terrible tales about what they might expect at the hands of these "vandals." Henry Hitchcock, one of Sherman's staff officers and a critical observer, remembered coming upon a Mrs. Elkins, "a regular Georgia woman" who used snuff and whose children were clay eaters, and noted in his diary how she "came to [the] gate in great fright, trying, poor woman, to hide it." She invited Sherman and his staff to come in, but her panic was evident. She told Sherman, as Hitchcock wrote it down, that "they were told before we came that we had been killing everybody and burning every house. This whole people seem to live on lies," Hitchcock bemoaned. When Sherman sent a staff member to Mrs. Elkins's smoke house to save the clothes she had buried there, and when one of Sherman's officers offered her some snuff, she decided that these Federals were not as brutish as she had been told. As her fear left her, she became friendlier, and she felt more confident in speaking her mind. She predicted that Savannah would fall "without a gun being fired."

More than a few women insisted that they really supported the Union cause, their men having been forced into the

Confederate service. "Very often when we have been destroying property," an Indiana doctor said, "the women would say
'Well, I don't care, if you will only serve South Carolina the
same way for they got us into this scrape." After the war,
Sherman reported a humorous example of feigned Union loyalty. A woman had just finished her tale of animosity toward the
Confederacy when a soldier ran by carrying a rooster in his
arms, with the woman's son close by on his heels. "Ma! Ma!
stop that man," the boy cried, "he's got Jeff Davis under his
arm."

In short, women, while frightened, frequently felt secure
enough to speak their minds and even offer physical resistance. They sometimes paid the price with a burned building
or destruction of some sort, but the Union soldiers usually
ignored them or shook their head in disbelief. Physical
reprisals simply were not within the soldiers' purview, much as
they wondered about the femininity of the many harsh women
they encountered and their certitude that the army's activities
would teach the southern ladies the error of their ways.

The main army columns were even more frightening than
the bummers on the flanks, if for no other reason than their
sheer size. As Sherman's troops approached, civilians frequently tried to get out of the way, taking whatever they could
with them. The arrival of the troops was a frightening specta-
cle, as a white Georgia woman aptly described in her diary,
"Like demons they rush in! To my smoke house, my dairy,
pantry kitchen and cellar . . . breaking locks and whatever is in
their way." The soldiers searched through everything inside
and outside the house, looking into hollow trees and logs and
every other possible hiding place. They were particularly suspicious of recently spaded dirt and often, by digging around in
such places, found treasure troves of food or valued posses-
sions that Georgians were trying to hide. Unfortunately, too,
they sometimes found that recently turned earth was the burial site of some unfortunate person or animal that had only

recently died. A Georgia woman, for example, told of a succession of soldiers digging up her recently buried dog four times.

The pillaging by soldiers in the main columns created an army unlike any other in American history. Hams and vegetables were strung around necks and moved rhythmically when the encumbered men walked. Chickens, both dead and alive, were everywhere, under arms, around necks, in makeshift cages, and dragged along the ground. Knapsacks and baskets overflowing with produce and other booty weighed heavily on marching shoulders. As the army moved forward, soldiers got tired of carrying extra weight and threw off the less appealing spoils, so that the roadsides became cluttered with refuse. Broken down horses and mules were summarily shot and replaced with better stock. The stink from decayed vegetables and animals was sometimes overwhelming.

Despite the amount of individual pillaging, brigade and division quartermasters retained the responsibility of feeding their units, and this meant refilling supply wagons as soon as they emptied. Sherman made sure that these wagons had the right of way among his marching troops, but the column did not wait for any wagon loading supplies along the way. If a wagon did not keep pace, it had to go to the rear of the column. The soldiers that the wagon supported had to wait in camp that night for necessary supplies, and sometimes suffer a late or no meal.

Union soldiers dealt with this problem by developing a system to fill wagons on the move. While marching they would pack the contents from all the wagons into one or two front wagons, thus providing six to ten empty vehicles. Then the quartermaster and his men would ride ahead of the column until they discovered some supplies. Leaving behind a guard at the site of the food, the quartermaster and his men would open a road to the newly discovered supplies and divert the empty wagons there, fill them up, and return them to their place in the moving column. Sherman remembered that, on one occasion, he saw something like ten wagons being loaded with corn from a crib "almost without stopping." The soldiers "raised the whole side of the crib, a foot or two; the wagons drove close alongside, and the men in the cribs, lying on their backs, kicked out a wagon-load of corn in the time I have taken to describe it," the general said approvingly.

The value of the goods, produce, and material taken in this manner and in less organized ways was prodigious. Historian Bruce Catton reported that soldiers in one regiment concluded that Sherman's army "must have accounted for one hundred thousand hogs, twenty thousand head of cattle, fifteen thousand horses and mules, five hundred thousand bushels of corn, and one hundred thousand bushels of sweet potatoes." Other statistics indicate that the army wrecked over three hundred miles of railroad track. In his memoirs, Sherman said he believed his army had done one hundred million dollars worth of destruction (over a billion dollars in early twenty-first century money). Others have provided an array of figures, but there is no way of ever finding out exactly how much destruction Georgia experienced during the march. But the devastation was enormous; the 1870 census showed that the value of farm land in Georgia was only about fifty percent of what it had been in 1860. The psychological impact on the people was even greater.

6

RESPONSIBILITY FOR
DESTRUCTION

There is no doubt that there was vast destruction during the march to the sea, but Sherman's army was not the sole agent of that destruction. Confederate leaders called upon Georgians to destroy goods and produce so that Sherman and the Union army could not benefit from Georgia's bounty, and some citizens followed these orders. A few Union army stragglers under no military discipline also pillaged. Numbers of southern civilians took advantage of the situation to get revenge or to make a profit, and former slaves contributed to the destruction. Even before Sherman's arrival, bands of southern marauders had already made life miserable for the region's people.

Wheeler's cavalry was particularly notorious for its pillaging activities, holding that reputation even before the Union army's entrance into Georgia. On November 16, the day

Sherman left Atlanta, Georgia Gov. Joe Brown had complained to Jefferson Davis's cabinet: "The houses, lands and effects of the people of Georgia are daily seized and appropriated to the use of the [Confederate] Government or its agents, without the shadow of law, without just compensation, and in defiance of the decision of the Supreme Judicial Tribune of the State; and the officers of justice are openly resisted by officers of the Confederate States."

Getting no satisfaction from the Richmond government, Brown issued his own proclamation on November 24, directly pointing his finger at Wheeler: "It is a matter of extreme mortification to know that a large part of our cavalry force . . . have left their commands and are now scattered in squads and small bands over nearly half of the territory of the State, robbing and plundering the citizens indiscriminately, and taking from the wives and children of soldiers who are in the service, discharging their whole duty, the supplies or provisions which are their only means of support." A Georgia civilian agreed. In a letter to the Confederate Secretary of War, this individual appealed "on behalf of the producing population of the states of Georgia and South Carolina, for protection against the destructive lawlessness of members of General Wheeler's command." The February 22, 1865, Richmond *Whig* even concluded "that our people would rather see the Yankees or Old Satan himself than a party of . . . Wheeler's cavalry."

There was, therefore, a plague of destruction taking place in Georgia, a great deal of it perpetrated by Sherman's army. Tom Gray, a University of Georgia historian, writing in 1930, concluded that "much of the property destroyed during the march was destroyed by the defenders." When Henry Hitchcock appeared at the house of a Mr. Loughborough twen ty days into the march, he found "inside the house everything in dire confusion - - - bureau drawers pulled out, furniture upset, books piled and tossed about," and the perpetrators, he learned, were not Sherman's men but Confederate soldiers.

Georgians knew very well who was responsible for the destruction, but, unlike Joe Brown, they hesitated to complain about their own soldiers. Sherman and his troopers, therefore, took the brunt of the criticism, some of it inaccurate propaganda. Slave owners told their servants that Sherman burned Atlanta to the ground and had locked black people inside buildings before torching them. A newspaper reported an alleged ball Sherman's officers had organized during the march, a gathering where, the paper said, the only attending women were black. In the same newspaper, there appeared an editorial accusing Union soldiers of raping southern white women claiming that one of the alleged victims became insane as a result.

The Georgia press regularly published articles predicting disaster for the invading Federals, accusing the intruders of a variety of transgressions. On November 20, the Augusta *Constitutionalist* insisted: "He is retreating — simply retreating. He will destroy, as he goes, but that makes it none the less so." Earlier, the Savannah *News* had written: "As Napoleon was forced to retreat from his conquest of Moscow, so is his feeble and heartless imitator, Sherman, forced to return from Atlanta." Since northern newspapers had no information from their own reporters because Sherman had excluded correspondents, anything found in the southern press was published. Before long, Northerners heard that "General Sherman was surrounded by Confederate troops, that his supplies were cut off, [and] that successful attacks had been made upon his scattered forces."

Soldiers in Georgia, when they came upon a newspaper reporting disaster for Sherman's army, only laughed. Henry Hitchcock, Sherman's staff member who felt very squeamish about the destruction the Union army perpetrated, grew even angrier at Confederate newspaper and civilian propaganda, "If any one thing is more despicable than another in these 'Southern chivalry' it is the infernal lies they spread about the 'Yanks,'—our uniform cruelty, our killing all the women and

HENRY HITCHCOCK

Henry Hitchcock: Born in Spring Hill, Alabama, in 1829, he was the son of the chief justice of the Alabama Supreme Court. His father's death in the early 1840s caused his mother to move the family to Tennessee, where Hitchcock graduated from the University of Nashville in 1846. He graduated from Yale College in 1848 and taught high school for a year in Worcester, Massachusetts before retuning to Nashville to study law in the office of the later chancellor of the Tennessee Supreme Court. In 1851, he moved to St. Louis, where he became a major city leader. He was immediately admitted to the bar, but for a year he helped edit a Whig newspaper before returning full time to the law. As a Republican, he supported Lincoln in the 1860 election and served in the state convention called to determine Missouri's relationship with the United States. He led the two year convention battle to keep Missouri in the Union. A pre-war acquaintance of Sherman's, he became his staff judge advocate beginning with the march to the sea. In April 1865, Sherman sent him to Washington with the text of his peace agreement with Confederate General Joseph E. Johnston. In the post-war era, Hitchcock was, for seven years, dean of the Washington University Law School, a leading civil attorney in St. Louis, the author of important legal writings, and in 1889-1890, the president of the American Bar Association, which he helped found. He was also one of the co-founders of the National Civil Service Reform League. He died in St. Louis in 1902. He and Sherman developed a close relationship during the war. Hitchcock considered Sherman "a man of genius," and Sherman said of him: "He is a lawyer and scholar and can draw up my rude thoughts. . . ."

children, burning all the houses, forcing the negroes into our army in the front rank of battle, etc., etc. Everywhere we go we find these stories have been systematically and persistently spread and are believed, even by intelligent people." Hitchcock added that, along with Sherman, he had just visited the sick wife and children of a Georgia man who believed such stories yet left his family to the mercy of the "horrid Yanks." Sherman personally calmed the panicked wife and crying children and soon had them talking to him like old friends, deflating the family's fears with the reality of his person.

But Sherman could not visit every Georgian, and his reputation for alleged savagery preceded him. Although most rumors were untrue, exaggerated stories of Yankee cruelty helped serve Sherman's goal. All the actions of the Union and Confederate armies, in fact, fulfilled Sherman's psychological purpose. The general was making this march of destruction to convince Southerners to stop fighting and rejoin the Union. Sherman was telling the men and women of the South by word and deed that if they did not give up the cause, they would suffer grievously. There was no safety in being a civilian—society in general would pay the price for continuing the war. So, when Sherman's own men pillaged, set fires, and took jewelry, as well as food, and when Wheeler's cavalry and Georgia civilians looted each other, the same message prevailed. War had become hard, and destruction would only get worse if Southerners did not stop the rebellion. The Confederate military had not been able to protect the state capital of Milledgeville from the heavy hand of the invader, so what hope was there for the ordinary citizen and his 200-acre farm in the path of the juggernaut? It was all very frightening, and that was exactly what Sherman wanted it to be.

7
MARCHING TOWARD MILLEN AND THE POWs

Under new orders issued on November 23, the Union army proceeded toward its next major destination, Millen. Slocum's left wing marched toward Sandersville, while Howard's right wing took roads to the south, but generally paralleled the Georgia Central Railroad. Kilpatrick's cavalry traveled as quickly as it could one hundred miles to Millen to rescue the Federal prisoners incarcerated there. Sherman now traveled with Alpheus Williams' XX Corps of Slocum's wing. The once cold, windy, and rainy weather was now beautiful, and one Southerner complained: "The Lord must be on the side of the Yankees, he sends them such weather."

The only Confederate opposition besides Wheeler's cavalry, consisted of the Milledgeville militia: around six hundred convicts and young boys. Brig. Gen. Harry Wayne, their commander, had plans to stop the Federal right wing at the Oconee

River, but quickly saw that defending the river would only cause the slaughter of his inferior force, so he ordered his troops to fall back. The Federals, unopposed, crossed the river on pontoon bridges.

Slocum's wing, with Sherman present, reached Sandersville on November 26. Skirmishers drove a brigade of Confederate cavalry into and through the town, the horse soldiers setting some fodder on fire. When Sherman entered Sandersville, he let it be known, in no uncertain terms, that if Georgia civilians or the Confederate military attempted to burn any more food in the Union army's path, he would intensify the destruction on the state. Meanwhile, Howard's wing arrived opposite its northern wing counterpart, exactly where Sherman wanted Howard's troops. The general's plan continued to unfold perfectly.

That evening, another black man came to see Sherman at his headquarters. Sherman asked the man whether any Federals had arrived in a small town, some six miles from Sandersville. "First there came along some cavalry-men, and they burned the depot," the man reported, "Then come along some infantry-men, and they tore up the track, and burned it." Then, he said to the incredulous Union commander, the soldiers "sot fire to the well." When Sherman rode into the town the next day, November 27, the general found Maj. John M. Corse's division, XIV Corps of Howard's right wing, still destroying the railroad. Sherman also discovered that the black man's description of the well burning was accurate. The well consisted of a square hole in the ground, some twenty-five feet deep, all boarded up and with wooden stairs to the bottom where a pump powered water to a tank above ground. The soldiers broke up the wood boarding, threw it into the well, and set it all on fire. The Union soldiers had indeed torched a well.

Sherman now accompanied Frank Blair's XVIII Corps of Howard's right wing. Kilpatrick and his cavalry on the left wing, moved quickly toward Waynesboro, located on a branch

(HUGH) JUDSON KILPATRICK

(Hugh) Judson Kilpatrick: Born in Deckertown, New Jersey, in 1836, Kilpatrick entered the United States Military Academy in 1856, at which time he dropped his first name. He graduated in 1861, seventeenth out of a class of forty-five. He immediately joined the 5th New York Infantry Regiment, a Zouave unit, as a captain. When  Kilpatrick was wounded at the battle of Big Bethel in June 1861, he became the first regular army officer wounded in the war. In September, he became a lieutenant colonel in a cavalry unity, the beginnings of his career as a horse soldier. By June of 1863 Kilpatrick was commanding a cavalry division in the Army of the Potomac, participating in all the major cavalry fights in the East and in Second Bull Run. In February 1864 he commanded the Kilpatrick-Dahlgren Raid, the unsuccessful attempt to capture Richmond, free prisoners of war, and distribute amnesty proclamations behind enemy lines. The raid was a miserable failure, and Col. Ulrich Dahlgren died in the effort along with over three hundred horse soldiers and a large number of horses. In April 1864, Grant sent Kilpatrick to the West, where he commanded a cavalry division in Sherman's Atlanta campaign, and was wounded in Resaca early in the campaign.

Kilpatrick returned to duty in July and participated in the march across Georgia and through the Carolinas, gaining the reputation as being the harshest officer in the invading Union forces. Kilpatrick resigned his commission in late 1865, and became United States minister to Chile until 1868. He supported Horace Greeley, the Liberal Republican-Democratic candidate for president in 1872 and was an unsuccessful Republican candidate for Congress in 1880. In 1881 Kilpatrick returned to his Chilean post, but died that same year, his body later being returned for burial at West Point. Kilpatrick's nickname was "Kill-cavalry," both because of his aggressive non-flinching style of warfare and because he regularly used up horses and demonstrated frequent lapses of judgement. He has a well-deserved reputation for woman-izing and was universally considered eccentric. Sherman kept him as his head of cavalry because, Sherman said: "I know that Kilpatrick is a hell of a damned fool, but I want just that sort of man to command my cavalry in this expedition."

railroad between Millen and Augusta. This movement was meant to continue to deceive the Confederates into believing that Sherman's army was planning an attack on Augusta. The only significant Confederate opposition remaining in the state consisted of the 10,000 men under William J. Hardee in Savannah and the marauding cavalry men of Joe Wheeler.

Disdainful of any serious resistance from the outnumbered and demoralized Confederates, Kilpatrick let his guard down. During the night of November 28, Wheeler's horse soldiers dashed into Kilpatrick's camp at Sylvan Grove, stole regimental colors and several dozen horses, and took some sleepy prisoners. Only partially dressed because he was in bed with a local woman, Kilpatrick had to jump fences on a saddle-less horse to escape the intruders. For the next several days, the two cavalry units battled each other near Augusta in the so-called battle of Waynesboro, the Confederates besting the northern troops.

Kilpatrick decided to call for help from the infantry, and two brigades of Union foot soldiers arrived. Kilpatrick put his entire division on line and then placed the infantry in a second line behind them. The general went on the attack and, much to his satisfaction, easily pushed Wheeler's horsemen off the field, inflicting some 300 casualties while suffering only fifty on his side. Kilpatrick continued to drive his force towards Waynesboro and then through the town until his troops reached Slocum's marching columns and fell in with them.

All did not always go smoothly for Union forces, however. Hoping to take advantage of the Confederate panic over Sherman's advancing army, Maj. Gen. John G. Foster, the commander of the Department of the South, then at Hilton Head, South Carolina, decided to send an army and navy contingent under Brig. Gen. John P. Hatch to capture the Savannah and Charleston Railroad, the main supply line for Savannah. The attempt was a fiasco. Union troops marched in the wrong direction, thus giving 1,400 Confederate troops under Gustavus W.

FRANK PRESTON BLAIR, JR.

Frank Preston Blair, Jr.: Born in Lexington, Kentucky, in 1821, the son of a leading Jacksonian newsman and later Republican leader, and the brother of Lincoln's Postmaster General, Blair was a graduate of Princeton University and Transylvania Law School. He entered law practice with his brother Montgomery in St. Louis in 1842. Having gone to New Mexico just prior to the outbreak of the Mexican war, Blair was appointed attorney general for the territory by Gen. Stephen Kearney after the American takeover. A leading opponent of the expansion of slavery into the territories, Blair served two terms in the Missouri legislature as a Free Soil Democrat, but later helped organize the Missouri Republican Party. He served four terms in Congress (1857-1859, 1860-1864). Blair served as chairman of the House Military Affairs Committee at the outset of the war and worked hard to gear up the Federal military machinery for the contest. He also took a leading role, with Brig. Gen. Nathaniel Lyon, to keep Missouri in the Union, serving temporarily as colonel, First Regiment, Missouri Volunteers. In the fall of 1862, Blair accepted a commission as brigadier general and recruited several divisions throughout the Midwest for the Vicksburg campaign. He steadily moved up in rank and responsibility, serving with Sherman during the Vicksburg campaign, Chattanooga, Atlanta, the march across Georgia, and then through the Carolinas. From January to April 1864 Blair regained a place in Congress, but his opponent successfully contested his seat. After the war, Blair returned to Missouri where he helped organize the Democratic party in opposition to "Radical Republican" policies. In 1866, his lease of a Louisiana cotton plantation turned out disastrously. He was the Democratic vice presidential candidate in 1868 and served in the United States Senate from 1871-1873. Blair died in St. Louis in 1875. One of the most talented of the political generals, Blair regularly irritated Sherman because of his political activities, but gained his respect for his military energy and courage. He did yeoman services for the Union both on the battlefield and in the political arena.

Smith of the ill-fated Georgia militia and a mixture of other units a chance to mobilize and set up a defense line at Honey Hill, near Grahamville, South Carolina. The Union troops, which included a large number of black soldiers, charged the well-entrenched Confederates for most of November 30. The Union army suffered 750 casualties to only one hundred Confederate losses. The railroad remained in Confederate control, the slaughter at Griswoldville had been repaid, but the soldiers in Sherman's marching army had not been affected nor stopped.

Sherman now traveled with Blair's XVII Corps of Howard's right wing which reached Millen on December 3, and he spent a day coordinating the activities of the other columns. As Sherman reached the two-thirds point of the planned march, everything remained in good order: Howard and the XV Corps were near Scarboro, south of the Ogeechee River; Slocum with Williams' XX Corps was four miles north of Millen at a place called Buckhead Church; and Jeff Davis's XIV Corps was ten miles north of Lumpkin's Station.

Five miles out of Millen along the Georgia Central Railroad, the soldiers found Camp Lawton, a substantial prisoner of war holding area. The more famous Camp Sumter at nearby Andersonville had been emptied and a large number of Union prisoners temporarily moved to Millen. Kilpatrick was unable to rescue the prisoners incarcerated in Millen, but had seen numbers of them, thin and worn, being loaded into box cars for transport out of the area. The empty prison was nothing more than a stockade pen about 300 yards square. According to Henry Hitchcock, there was "no shelter of any kind, no shed, nor tent, nor roof whatever, in any weather." There was also no source of water inside the enclosure except for some swamp area, but there were around 700 unmarked graves and several unburied corpses. When George Barnard, the famous photographer who had only that day caught up with Sherman after taking photographs at Atlanta, saw the stockade, he boiled with anger, "I used to be much troubled about the burning of houses, etc., but after what I have seen I shall not be much troubled about it." Hitchcock surmised, "How do those feel who have suffered in it! The burned houses, in spite of orders, are the answer."

Federal soldiers were enraged, as was Sherman himself. According to a colonel, the general ordered Frank Blair "to make the destruction 'ten fold more devlish' than he had ever dreamed of." Union troops did not need any encouragement, and many took action on their own. A number of soldiers, including some who had once been prisoners in Millen and had been refused the purchase of a meal at the local hotel, set a huge fire at the rear of the establishment. As the fire reached its zenith and began spreading to the main part of the building, someone noticed that a local woman with severe mental illness was missing and was feared trapped inside the building. Hitchcock and several other staff members ran in to try to find her, only to learn that she was in the garden aimlessly caressing a large goose. As the hotel burned, Hitchcock gave a black woman some money to take care of the mentally ill woman until other help arrived. The curious mix of anger and empathy continued to exist in Sherman's army.

8
THE BLACK MARCHERS

The rich countryside provided all the army needed as it moved through Georgia to Milledgeville. As the columns left Millen, what had once been productive farm land became barren lowlands, sandy and then, near Savannah, swampy. Near the end of the march, flooded rice fields replaced corn and other grain crops. The soldiers ate rice instead of their more usual fare, and since the food was new to the northern troops, they had to learn how to hull it before they could even begin eating the new provision. Some soldiers went hungry before they caught on to the technique. An officer told his men when they complained of their hunger, "Well, boys, the only thing I can advise is to draw in your belt one more hole each day."

The resulting scarcity of food from Millen to the ocean made the army grow increasingly exasperated about the ever larger number of slaves joining the march. Estimated numbers of contrabands range from ten thousand to twenty-five thousand people in all. Despite repeated Confederate claims that

A sketch depicting the number of contrabands following Sherman's army.

slaves were content in their servitude, huge numbers of former slaves left their owners behind and followed Sherman's army to the sea. As it developed, Sherman freed more slaves than any other Civil War general. He continued conferring with the black people found around the army, repeatedly telling them to remain in place. The Union army did not have enough food to feed the soldiers and the freedmen. The black followers listened, and some took his advice, but huge numbers continued to view the Union general and his soldiers as their only hope of salvation. The former slaves feared their fate at the hands of angry Confederate soldiers and civilians who were frustrated at the advance of Sherman's army.

All along the way, therefore, despite Sherman's lectures, when the army moved, the contrabands moved, too, stoically trudging along toward what they were sure was the day of jubilee. When the soldiers camped for the night, the runaways

A picture showing former slaves who followed the Union army across Georgia.

camped nearby. Surrounding the army campfires were the makeshift bivouacs of the fleeing slaves and the variety of animals and goods they brought with them. Most of Sherman's soldiers had little knowledge of black people, slave or free, so their reaction to them was enormously varied. Some troops were racists, others abolitionists. Most were not sure how they felt. The soldiers slipped food to the slaves, played tricks on them, physically abused them, and ransacked the contrabands' meager property. The troops also enjoyed black music, used the black population for intelligence, and, in the cases of children and attractive women, viewed them as pets and prostitutes. As had been the case in slavery, the treatment of black people varied according to the whims and character of the whites who had control over their destinies.

At first, the slaves showed excitement at the coming of the Union army and warmly greeted the soldiers as their deliverers from bondage. Eventually, however, the black population

JEFFERSON C. DAVIS

Jefferson C. Davis: Born in Clark Country, Indiana, in 1828, Davis enlisted as a private in the Mexican War and received a direct commission in the artillery in 1848. Davis was stationed at Fort Sumter during the Confederate attack on the installation and became a captain soon after. He steadily rose through the ranks, participating as a division commander at Pea Ridge in March 1862, and Corinth in May 1862. In September 1862 while organizing Louisville, Kentucky's defenses, Davis and William Bull Nelson, his commanding officer, became engaged in a shouting match at the Galt House Hotel. Davis went for a pistol and fatally shot Nelson. His friendship with Indiana Gov. Oliver P. Morton saved him from prosecution, and soon Davis returned to military duty. He was a division commander at Stones River, Chickamauga, the Atlanta campaign, and a corps commander during the march through Georgia and the Carolinas. Because of the slaying of Nelson and the controversial drowning of former slaves at Ebenezer Creek, Davis never received the promotions he might have otherwise gained. He made major general only by brevet. In the post-war years, Davis held a military post in Alaska and participated in the punitive campaign against the Modoc Indians for the 1873 killing of Gen. Edward Canby. He died in Chicago in 1879 and is buried in Indianapolis. Controversial all his life, Davis also had the misfortune to have the same name, except for the middle initial, as the president of the Confederate States.

became less enthusiastic when faced with the variety of ill treatment they encountered. As historian Edmund Drago phrased it: "For some the millennium had become a nightmare." Some runaways returned crestfallen to plantations. Yet, huge numbers of former slaves endured the Union army's abuse and followed the Federals to what they believed was freedom.

No matter how northern troops treated the former slaves, many in Sherman's army, including the commander, looked upon them as a dangerous encumbrance. Racism played a role, of course, but Sherman was determined from the start of the campaign to prevent any impediment to his army, whether it be newspaper correspondents, humanitarians, outside medical personnel, or non-military people of any kind. The general wanted all non-soldiers to stay away from the army.

Sherman complained constantly, but took no concrete action to thwart the pursuing slaves. Still, according to Jacob D. Cox, a Sherman subordinate and post-war historian, "when the lower and less fruitful lands were reached, the embarrassment and military annoyance increased." On December 9, 1864, just twenty miles from Savannah, Jefferson C. Davis, commander of the XIV Corps in Slocum's left wing, an individual many troops disliked for his uncompromising irascibility, took action against some former slaves, a decision that ended in tragedy.

The column was moving along a causeway through a thick woods. Using a pontoon bridge, Davis's men were crossing Ebenezer Creek, a brackish body of water some thirty to forty yards wide, too deep and wide to ford. Davis's men were at the rear of Slocum's wing and behind them came 650 freedmen, including a large number of women and children. The 58th Indiana Regiment was the last of Davis's units to cross the bridge. The followers strained forward to be in position to cross with the troops, but, under direct orders from Davis, a guard of soldiers held them back. As the guard mounted the bridge, and the slaves prepared to follow, the soldiers suddenly dislodged the pontoons and floated them across to the other side. The black people were left on the shore, gasping in dismay.

John F. Hight, chaplain of the 58th Indiana, left a riveting, soul wrenching account of what happened next. The slaves, crowded on the shore, let out "a cry of agony," he said, and panicked at being left behind to the mercy of Wheeler's cavalry. The panic was noticeably evident to the chaplain watching from the opposite shore. Suddenly someone yelled out

"Rebels." There was "a wild rush," people diving into the water, hoping, in their desperation, to swim the unfordable water and get away from Wheeler's cavalrymen. Others ran up and down the bank, uncertain what to do, seeing danger before and behind. In the water, some of the desperate people made it to the other side, but some thrashing women and children began to drown.

The soldiers had already packed the deflated pontoons into the waiting wagons, but, appalled at what they saw, tried to help the desperate slaves. The troops threw logs and anything that would float into the water, and chopped several trees down, trying to span the creek. The slaves tried to make rafts out of the material, and a few more people made it across the creek, but many more drowned in the attempt. Meanwhile, the followers continued to press against the edge of the water, hoping to get across before the Confederate horsemen arrived.

When Wheeler's men did appear, they fired a few shots and then rode away. Davis's soldiers had moved on by this time, and the former slaves were left to their own devices. Some more made it across, while others drowned. Many more remained on the far shore. When Wheeler returned, his troops captured those who stayed behind, no doubt marching them back to slavery. According to the 58th Indiana physician, there was "great indignation among the troops." Personally, the doctor would have hanged Davis "as high as Haman," but, in any case, "I should not wonder if the valiant murderers of women and children should meet with an accident before long." The chaplain was equally upset. Hight called the incident "a scene disgraceful to American history," and characterized Davis as "a military tyrant, without one spark of humanity in his make-up."

Sherman, however, defended Davis, claiming that it was all an accident resulting from the former slaves disobeying his orders to stay away. In his memoirs, Sherman said that Davis "was strictly a soldier" who sympathized with the slaves, as all the soldiers did, but he "doubtless hated to have his wagons and columns encumbered" by them. Jacob Cox reflected Sherman's defensive attitude when he wrote: "It would be unjust to that officer [Jeff Davis] to believe that the order would have been given, if the effect had been foreseen."

About the same time of the Ebenezer Creek episode, a torpedo (land mine) blew off the leg of a young Union officer, a member of the 1st Alabama Cavalry, Blair's XVII Corps of Howard's right wing. Sherman was traveling with Blair's unit, and he and his staff were riding through a field when they noticed a commotion on a nearby road. They found the injured officer, his foot blown off below the ankle. The young man was lying under a blanket on the side of the road, waiting for a surgeon to amputate the damaged limb. Sherman became furious at learning that there were other mines buried in the area. No fighting had been reported in the vicinity, "nothing to give warning of danger." Sherman later wrote in his memoirs, "This was not war, but murder, and it made me very angry."

About this time, there arrived some Confederate prisoners of war, whom Corps commander Frank Blair ordered forward to dig up the rest of the mines. Two of these men pleaded with Sherman to rescind the order, but he angrily refused. As Henry Hitchcock recorded it, Sherman "told them their people had put these things there to assassinate our men instead of fighting them fair, and they must remove them; and if <u>they</u> got blown up he didn't care."

Union soldiers grew even angrier, expressed by Hitchcock as, "These cowardly villains call us 'barbarous Yankees'—and then adopt instruments of murder in cold blood where they dare not stand and fight like men. Torpedoes at the entrance to a fort are perhaps justifiable, for the fort itself is a warning. But here they run away, refuse to defend the road, but leave hidden in an open public road, without warning or chance of defense, these murderous instruments of assassination—contrary to every rule of civilized warfare." "These rebs are certainly insane," Hitchcock concluded, "their torpedoes could at most kill a few of our advance guard—could not possibly delay or interfere with such an army,—and they *know* must inevitably exasperate our men! *Quos Deus vult perdere prius dementat.*" (Those whom God would condemn, he first makes mad.)

9
SAVANNAH AND THE SEA

By December 10, 1864, Sherman's army reached the entrenchments guarding Savannah, Slocum's wing's left flank on the Savannah River, and Howard's wing spreading out to the right, the XV Corps on the furthest flank. Sherman's army was only four to five miles outside the city, having traveled over three hundred miles in twenty-four days. As he always did, Sherman immediately undertook a reconnaissance of the area. He and his escorts rode down the Louisville Road into a dense woods, where they left the horses and walked onto a railroad track located in a four foot cut. The tracks ran straight into Savannah. About half a mile away, Sherman could see an entrenched artillery battery. He warned the soldiers with him to expect to come under fire. The general saw a puff of smoke and watched the incoming cannon ball. He stepped out of the way, but a black man, crossing the track at the same time, did not react to the shouts of danger. A thirty-two pound cannon ball struck the ground and then caught the man under his chin

WILLIAM J. HARDEE

William J. Hardee: Born in Camden County, Georgia, in 1815, Hardee graduated from the United States Military Academy in 1838, twenty-sixth out of a class of forty-five. In the 1840s, he attended cavalry school in Paris, France, served in the Seminole War in Florida, and distinguished himself during the Mexican War. Encouraged by Secretary of War Jefferson Davis, Hardee published, in 1855, a manual entitled *Rifle and Light Infantry Tactics*. This text, normally called *Hardee's Tactics,* became the bible for officers on both sides of the Civil War. In 1856, Hardee became commandant of West Point. When Georgia seceded from the Union Hardee resigned his commission in the United States Army, and the Confederate States named him brigadier general that June and major general in October 1861. After a brief time in Arkansas, Hardee joined Albert Sidney Johnston at Shiloh and then Braxton Bragg at Perryville as corps commander. Made lieutenant general in October 1862, Hardee fought at Stones River and Chattanooga. He respected Joseph E. Johnston but could not get along with Braxton Bragg or John Bell Hood. Hardee took part in the Atlanta Campaign,  but because of problems with Hood, transferred to the Atlantic coast. The Confederate general could not prevent Sherman's march through Georgia or the Carolinas, and Hardee rejoined Johnston to participate in the failed Confederate attack at Bentonville. He surrendered with Johnston in April 1865. After the war, Hardee returned to his wife's plantation in Alabama, where he worked in both the insurance and the railroad businesses. He died while traveling to Virginia in 1873 and is buried in Selma, Alabama. Nicknamed "Old Reliable," Hardee was considered one of the Confederacy's premier corps commanders, but, when offered command of the Army of Tennessee after its loss of Chattanooga, Hardee refused, and was never asked again. Hardee never held command of a major Confederate army.

on the first bounce, tearing off his head. Sherman and his men covered the dead man with a blanket and then quickly departed out of range.

Sherman knew he had a serious problem and recalled, "We had again run up against the old familiar parapet, with its deep ditches, canals and bayous, full of water; and it looked as though another siege was inevitable." There were about 22,000 people in Savannah, the city on the Georgia side of the Savannah River built forty feet above the water on the closest inhabitable land from the ocean, about fifteen miles inland. The terrain outside the city and toward the ocean was almost at sea level and dominated by the salt marshes. With rice plantations and marshes bordering them, the Savannah and Ogeechee Rivers were only ten to fifteen miles apart beginning fifty miles inland and flowing to the ocean. The roads into Savannah consisted of five causeways, built above the wet lands and flooded rice plantations, two for railroads, and one each, for the Augusta, Louisville, and Ogeechee dirt roads. The dams, canals, and flood gates were man-made devices for flooding the rice fields. The flood gates had an obvious military value in time of attack, and William J. Hardee, the city's defender, stood ready to use them to his advantage.

Fort Pulaski, a major installation defending the city from ocean approach, had fallen into Union hands in 1862, so Confederate defenses against Federal naval vessels were restricted. The defenses consisted of a series of forts and redoubts within three miles of the city. Hardee could not depend solely on this interior line because then he would have to abandon the railroad to Charleston, his only sure source of outside supply. Therefore, Hardee decided long ago to defend the railroad bridge some fifteen to eighteen miles out of the city. As Sherman had marched toward Savannah, however, the Union army came in contact with Hardee's bridge-protecting defenses. Sherman's forces easily outflanked these works, and forced Hardee to fall back. Consequently by December 10, Hardee was within Savannah's interior fortifications. The only Confederate contact with Charleston and supply sources north was the Union Causeway to Hardeeville, South Carolina, six miles from the river and the only safe terminus of the Charleston Railroad. The situation for Hardee and Savannah was obviously grave.

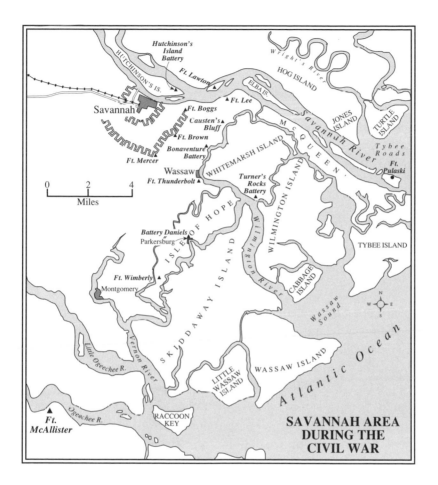

Hutchinson's
Island
Battery
HUTCHINSON'S IS.
Ft. Lawton
Wright's River
HOG ISLAND
ELBA IS
Ft. Lee
Savannah
Ft. Boggs
Causten's
Bluff
Ft. Brown
Bonaventure
Battery
Ft. Mercer
Wassaw
Ft. Thunderbolt
WHITEMARSH ISLAND
Turner's
Rocks
Battery
Savannah River
JONES
ISLAND
TURTLE
ISLAND
Tybee
Roads
Ft.
Pulaski
McQUEEN'S
WILMINGTON ISLAND
Wilmington River
CABBAGE
ISLAND
TYBEE ISLAND
ISLE OF HOPE
Battery Daniels
Parkersburg
Ft. Wimberly
Montgomery
SKIDDAWAY ISLAND
Wassaw
Sound
Atlantic Ocean
Vernon River
Little Ogeechee R.
Ft.
McAllister
Ogeechee R.
RACCOON
KEY
LITTLE
WASSAW
ISLAND
WASSAW ISLAND
Atlantic Ocean

0   2   4
Miles

N
W   E
S

**SAVANNAH AREA
DURING THE
CIVIL WAR**

Hardee's defenders consisted of 10,000 troops, and not all
of them regular soldiers. At the same time, however, Sherman
had run out of terrain to forage. The marshlands provided little
food, besides rice, and the Union general could not take the
time to besiege Savannah. Nevertheless on December 10,
1864, by Special Field Orders No. 130, Sherman gave specific
orders for the investiture of the city and to "open up communication with our fleet in Ossabaw and Wassaw Sounds" in the
Atlantic ocean. Sherman's army could not sustain the siege,
however, if necessary provisions did not arrive. Supply wagons

had rapidly emptied as the foraging areas became used up. The Federal supply situation was dire.

On December 12, Rear Admiral John A. Dahlgren, commander of the South Atlantic Blockading Squadron, telegraphed President Lincoln of "the great satisfaction of conveying to you information of the arrival of General Sherman, near Savannah, with his army in fine spirits." Dahlgren had earlier received word from a scout Gen. O.O. Howard had sent to the fleet. Learning this news, Lincoln breathed a sigh of relief.

Like everyone else, the president had not heard anything from or about Sherman as the general and his army had disappeared in the Georgia countryside. Sherman had been that successful in keeping information from reaching the outside world. The general could have sent regular news out, since he had telegraphers who systematically tapped telegraph lines to intercept Confederate messages, but Sherman chose instead not to send word of his progress to the North. When the Union army began the march on November 15, 1864, only eight to ten reporters had accompanied his army. His animosity toward reporters was well known, and newspaper correspondents knew to stay away. They also knew Sherman had become extremely effective at keeping reporters from getting their stories back to northern papers, and the thrust of the march meant that censorship would be even more severe than normal.

Northern newspapers, therefore, had little to report as Sherman had marched through Georgia. Papers reprinted Confederate press articles full of threats against the invaders and about Sherman's alleged imminent defeat, but kept warning northern readers that the words were nothing more than southern propaganda. The general public worried anyway. Repeatedly northern newspapers printed: "No news from Sherman today." Consequently, Northerners, including the president himself, did not know exactly where Sherman was and how the army fared. One day, Lincoln asked politician A.K. McClure, a newsman himself, if he would not like to know

An example of the defenses surrounding Fort McAllister.

Sherman's location. Thinking he had a scoop, McClure said he certainly would. "Well I'll be hanged if I wouldn't myself," Lincoln laughed in reply. Another time when John Sherman, the general's brother and a Republican senator from Ohio, asked the president if he had heard anything from Sherman in Georgia, Lincoln replied that he had not, "I know the hole he went in at, but I can't tell you what hole he'll come out of." Thus to learn from the navy that Sherman had finally arrived in Savannah sent a wave of relief across Washington and the northern states.

Unless Sherman could establish a sure supply line, however, the army was in peril. It became clear to the general that his best hope of establishing a new line of supplies was to capture Fort McAllister on the south bank of the Ogeechee River overlooking the entrance from Ossawbaw Sound, some twelve miles south of Savannah. Once this fort was captured, the

WILLIAM B. HAZEN

William B. Hazen: Born in West Hartford, Vermont, in 1830, Hazen moved to Ohio at the age of three where he became friends with later President James A. Garfield. Hazen graduated from the United States Military Academy at West Point in 1855, twenty-eight out of a class of thirty-four. He served with the infantry on the Pacific coast and in Texas. In 1859 he suffered a severe head wound during a battle with the Comanches in Texas and spent the next two years recuperating. When secession came, Hazen was promoted to captain in the 8th Infantry Regiment. In the fall of 1861, he became colonel of the 41st Ohio and during the battle of Shiloh, Hazen commanded a brigade in Don Carlos Buell's Army of the Ohio. He then fought at Corinth and Perryville. Hazen became brigadier general in April 1863 and participated in all the major western battles, leading a brigade and then a division during Sherman's Atlanta Campaign. He held this command during the marches to the sea and through the Carolinas, although Hazen did not gain a major generalship until the war's last days. The rank when given, however, dated from the day Hazen's troops had captured Fort McAllister, an act which endeared him to Sherman. After the war, Hazen held corps command from late May until August 1, 1865. He then served as regimental commander in the West and was instrumental in providing evidence against U.S. Grant's Secretary of War, William Belknap, in the corrupt army trading post scandal. In 1880, Hazen became the Army's chief signal officer, a post he retained until his death in Washington in 1887. Hazen wrote widely in the post-war years on military topics.

army could open communications with the U.S. Navy. Kilpatrick and his cavalrymen probed the installation earlier and found it too strong for cavalry attack, so Sherman discussed the matter with O.O. Howard, commander of the right wing. They decided to make an infantry assault.

The unit chosen for the December 13 attack on Fort McAllister was the second division of Osterhaus's XV Corps of Howard's wing, a unit commanded by William B. Hazen and once led by Sherman himself at Shiloh. The commanding general spoke to Hazen personally, "I explained to General Hazen, fully, that on his action depended the safety of the whole army, and the success of the campaign." Sherman and his staff then rode down the left side of the river to the Cheves Plantation where Howard's men built a signal/watch tower on top of a rice mill, allowing Union leaders a view of the lower Ogeechee. This tower was about three miles from Fort McAllister, which Sherman could clearly see across the salt marches.

Sherman and his staff climbed on the roof of a building attached to the rice mill, from where the signal officer in the tower above could contact the officers below. The observers could see the lower Ogeechee River and Ossabaw Sound beyond the clearly visible Fort McAllister. Hurried activity at the fort and some artillery firing inland indicated that Hazen had arrived and was preparing his attack. The signal officer soon gained visual contact with Hazen. The division commander asked if Sherman was present and, when told yes, reported that the attack would take place before nightfall. "The sun was rapidly declining," Sherman later reported, "and I was dreadfully impatient."

To add to the excitement and confusion, a ship appeared on the river, quickly recognized as part of the Union squadron. "Our attention was divided between this approaching steamer and the expected assault," Sherman said. Another message from Hazen reported that the Union forces were prepared to begin the assault, and Sherman ordered them to do so immediately because the approaching Union ship could distract the defenders. Meanwhile, officers on the steamer, using a signal flag, asked "Who are you?" "General Sherman" was signaled back. "Is Fort McAllister taken?" the ship's officers asked further. "Not yet," Sherman replied, "but it will be in a minute!" Just then, at 5 P.M., Hazen's troops came out of the woods ringing the fort. One observer stated, "the lines dressed as on parade, with colors flying, and moving forward with a quick, steady pace." One line attacked from below the fort, another from above, and a third from the rear. The lines moved simultaneously, passing through an abatis, over deadly torpedoes, through a fifteen foot deep ditch with five to six feet high stakes set in its seven foot wide bottom. Heavy guns fired at the charging attackers. Each line reached the parapet about the same time, and the heavy artillery fort fell to the charging Union soldiers in about fifteen minutes. Federal forces suffered only twenty-four killed and one hundred wounded, mostly from torpedoes, while the garrison suffered forty-eight dead with the rest of the 250 defenders wounded or captured.

All eyes at the rice mill observation tower alternated their view between the fighting at the fort and Sherman's expressions. Peering through his field glasses, the commanding general was nervously animated, "Look, Howard, look! Magnificent! See that flag, how steadily it advances! Not a man falters - Grand! Grand!" When the attack seemed to hesitate, "he took down his glass as if unable to witness the failure." But the hesitation was only temporary, and the men were soon on top of the parapet and then inside the fort. McAllister was taken, and Sherman was ecstatic, "Howard, Savannah is mine!" And then as Sherman remembered it in his memoirs, "I exclaimed, in the language of the poor negro at Cobb's plantation, 'This nigger will have no sleep this night!'" One of his aides noticed, too, that Sherman "was so delighted & so stirred up . . . that he absolutely <u>cried</u>."

In his excitement, Sherman ran down to the wharf near the rice mill, and several young officers there volunteered to row him and General Howard to the fort. At an overseer's house nearby, Sherman found the victorious Union officers eating dinner and "congratulated Hazen most heartily on his brilliant success and praised its execution very highly as it deserved." After joining in the meal and hearing all about the assault, Sherman and a party of officers visited McAllister itself. When they arrived, a sentry warned them about torpedoes, just as a land mine blew apart a soldier trying to find a wounded or dead friend.

After completing his investigation of the fort, Sherman decided to deliver news of McAllister's capture to the fleet himself. There was a yawl in the river nearby which Sherman and Howard boarded, ignoring the danger from torpedoes in the water. The ship that Sherman had seen from his rice plantation vantage point was now nowhere on the horizon, but he later spied it ahead as the steamer was returning to the fleet. Sherman helped row the small boat out to the Union fleet. When the steamer was reached, Sherman, Howard, and the navy officers exchanged warm greetings and war stories. Sherman learned that, thankfully, there were nearby supplies ready for his army. He also learned that Grant was still besieging Petersburg. After obtaining some writing paper, Sherman wrote to Grant and Stanton, reporting his success. Then Sherman visited Adm. John Dahlgren, commander of the South Atlantic Blockading Squadron and Maj. Gen. J.G. Foster, commander of the Department of the South. Sherman established his headquarters with Howard's wing about eight miles from Savannah. Since the fall of Fort McAllister opened a supply line to the army, Sherman now determined to invest Savannah until it fell. He moved expeditiously to tighten the noose around the city.

On December 15, the army received the best present it could wish for, letters from home. Having been cut off from the outside world for a month, the men were happy to learn what they had missed while marching through Georgia. Sherman, however, received a letter from Grant dated December 6 which he did not find exhilarating. Grant had worried about Sherman throughout the march, comparing him to "a ground mole when he disappears under a lawn. You can here and there trace his track, but you are not quite certain where he will come out till you see his head." Happy to see Sherman emerge, Grant offered congratulations, told Sherman to secure a good base on the ocean, leave a

ULYSSES S. GRANT

Ulysses S. Grant: Born in Point Pleasant, Ohio, in 1822, Grant's original name was Hiram Ulysses. When a congressman mistakenly put Ulysses Simpson (his mother's maiden name) on his application to the United States Military Academy, he gained a new name. Cadets called him  Sam, and later he became famous as U.S. Grant. He graduated from West Point in 1843, twenty-first out of a class of thirty-nine. During the Mexican War, Grant had great admiration for Gen. Zachary Taylor, though he won battle distinction while serving under Winfield Scott. Ordered to the Pacific Coast after the war, he began to drink because of loneliness for his wife, resulting in his decision to resign his commission in July 1854. He was a failure as a civilian, and finally returned to his home town of Galena, Illinois, to work for the family business. When secession came, it was only with the aid of Congressmen Elihu B. Washburne that Grant gained a post in the army. Grant's career took off quickly, however. He gained national prominence with his "unconditional surrender" victory at Fort Donelson in February 1862. Though accused of allowing his forces to be surprised at Shiloh in April 1862, Grant's determined counter attack on the second day of the battle drove the Confederates back to Corinth. His masterful campaign for Vicksburg in the spring and summer of 1863 marked him as one of the great military leaders of the conflict. Grant quickly gained overall command of the western theater of the war and relived the Confederate siege of Chattanooga in November 1863. Raised to the rank of lieutenant general in March 1864, Grant became commander of all Union armies and moved East to direct the Army of the Potomac's eventual victory over Robert E. Lee's Army of Northern Virginia. He was promoted to full general and held overall army command until 1869 when he became president of the United States for two terms. He later suffered repeated financial reverses and fought his last battle against his most fatal enemy, throat cancer, which claimed victory over him in 1885. Grant's memoirs, completed just before his death, were one of the most successful books ever published and left his family financially secure after his death. An unimpressive looking man, Grant had the ability to plot strategy that encompassed the continent and recognized the changing nature of war. He had a decisiveness that allowed him to react to battle field conditions calmly and surely. Where other generals might retreat, Grant continued pressing forward.

garrison to defend it, and then "with the balance of your command come here [to Virginia] by water with all dispatch." "I have concluded that the most important operation toward closing the rebellion will be to close out Lee and his army."

Sherman was stunned at this news. Conventional warfare such as Grant was fighting in Virginia was undesirable to Sherman. He had shown in this march, he believed, that there was a better way to fight than through pitched battles which resulted in huge casualties. By bringing the war to the populace and terrorizing them with destruction, the Union army could end the war more quickly than by fighting bloody battles. Besides, Sherman wanted to capture Savannah; the march would be incomplete without its capitulation. Despite his unhappiness, however, the general promised to obey Grant's order and began converting Fort McAllister into the supply base per Grant's instruction. Sherman realized, however, that it would take time to gather the necessary ships to transport his army to Virginia, so he decided to capture Savannah before departing the region.

He wrote a letter to Hardee on December 17 demanding his surrender, but the Confederate refused. Sherman continued tightening the siege. Significantly, however, he left Hardee one escape route—across the Savannah River, east of the city. Union soldiers found this situation strange, but quickly they realized Sherman's plan. According to one Union officer, the army "concluded [that] Sherman wanted the enemy to leave and not make a fight necessary." They were correct; Sherman did not desire a fight. Instead, his aim continued to be the infliction of all the devastation necessary to convince the Confederate army and its people to quit the war. Destroy rather than kill. This idea dominated Sherman's thinking and explained his willingness to let Hardee and his soldiers escape from Savannah.

On December 20, 1864, after destroying the navy yard, two ironclads, some smaller ships, and a great deal of ordnance

A photograph of one of Savannah's various waterways.

and ammunition, Hardee and his 10,000 soldiers morosely took the escape route Sherman had left open to them and crossed the Savannah River into South Carolina on a shaky bridge of hastily assembled rice flats. Savannah with its 250 heavy guns and over 30,000 bales of cotton lay open to the Union army. Three weeks earlier, on November 30, in Tennessee, Maj. Gen. John A. Schofield had defeated John Bell Hood and his Army of Tennessee at the battle of Franklin. Then Schofield's troops linked up with George H. Thomas to cripple the Confederate army fatally at the battle of Nashville on December 15 and 16. Sherman was thrilled at this great victory and sent congratulations to Thomas. "I do not believe your own wife was more happy at the result than I was," he said, secure that the victory at Nashville had vindicated his decision of "taking away so large a proportion of the army" for the march. Meanwhile, Sherman convinced Grant that his forces

FRANK LESLIE'S ILLUSTRATED NEWSPAPER.

SANTA CLAUS SHERMAN PUTTING SAVANNAH INTO UNCLE SAM'S STOCKING.

A cartoon depicting Sherman's "present" of
Savannah to President Lincoln.

could reach Virginia on foot as quickly as they could sail there
and that his men would be in better shape to fight if they
walked rather than sailed. Here was a confident, even brash
general. Everywhere he turned, Sherman had been successful.
His brand of war worked. "This may seem a hard species of
warfare," he said in his January 1, 1865, report on the march,
"but it brings the sad realities of war home to those who have
been directly or indirectly instrumental in involving us in its
attendant calamities."

When Sherman rode into Savannah on December 21, he
found a city of beautiful homes, built around a series of tree
and bush filled squares, entered into from broad streets. The
Savannah *Republican*, which like all southern newspapers had
ridiculed and castigated Sherman's forces, on December 21
called for the city's populace to act in such a way as to gain
the "respect of a magnanimous foe." Sherman had consistently

said that he would fight a hard war but administer a soft peace. He had implemented destruction to the level of a winning war strategy, and now he stood ready to utilize soft peace to the same effect. He wrote Abraham Lincoln on December 22 and electrified the North, "I beg to present to you, as a Christmas present, the city of Savannah."

He felt generous toward the city's fourteen thousand whites and eight thousand five hundred blacks. He found Savannah's citizens and their governmental authorities properly humbled, calling them "the worst whipped and subjugated [individuals] you ever saw." The fact that the mayor and city alderman paid him a respectful visit and that leading Confederate officers, William J. Hardee, Gustavus W. Smith, Lafayette McLaws, and A.P. Stewart had left their wives in his care was flattering and indicated that they did not believe the horror stories that other Confederates had spread about him and his march. Sherman was ready to show Savannah and the rest of the South that he had always been serious when he had promised generosity if only they stopped fighting.

The foraging bummers of the march now became the polite gentlemen of Savannah, intrigued by the city, the water all around it, and the oysters they gobbled down with abandon. Whenever soldiers came into town from the surrounding camps, they paid for everything they needed or wanted instead of simply taking things as they had done during the march. The Union army also brought law and order back to Savannah by putting an end to the plundering of stores and houses by some of the city's citizens, women included. Sherman used his contacts in the North to stimulate economic activity in the city. He had his favorite regimental band play public concerts, and he overwhelmed the people by staging an impressive military parade two days before Christmas. Sherman even shocked his own soldiers when he put aside his usual plain outfit and wore "the full-dress uniform of a major general with stars and gold braid and tassels, and flashing accouterments." "Uncle Billy's dolled up like a duke," one surprised soldier whispered to another.

To an unbelieving public, convinced by Confederate propaganda that Sherman was a brute of the worst kind, his soft peace and his pleasant manner were a shock. Some Savannah residents maintained a sullen silence, refusing to warm up to the man who had conquered their state so completely and destructively. Others gave a grudging nod to him. The founder of the Girl Scouts of America, Juliette Low, was then a young girl, and her mother, Eleanor Kinzie Gordon, remembered how Sherman had charmed the suspicious little girl and her sister when he visited their home. He put one on his knee, placed his arm around the other, Gordon said, "and he kept them in shouts of laughter till long past their bedtime." Sherman was pleased. "There are some very elegant people here, whom I knew in better days and who do not seem ashamed to call on the 'vandal chief,'" he said. He reminisced with these people about those good old days and how it felt "strange . . . to lead a large army through this land," where as a young officer he had experienced such good times. "I pledge you," he told an old woman friend "that my study is to accomplish peace and honor at as small a cost to life and property as possible."

At first, Sherman stayed at the Pulaski House, where he had lived when stationed in the city as a young officer before the war. After a visit from the mayor, who ironically was the departed General Hardee's brother, Sherman met Charles Green, a wealthy British banker, who insisted that the general stay at his beautiful house on Madison Square. This two story mansion, furnished with fine art and with banana trees growing in indoor tubs, was considered one of the city's finest residences. It provided luxurious living, particularly when compared to the open air camping on the march. Here on Christmas Day, Sherman, with Green's enthusiastic support, hosted a dinner for some twenty of his officers, and later Sherman hosted what he called a "social gathering" for some

A sketch of Sherman's parade through Savannah.

one hundred officers and civilians. The two newspapers Sherman allowed to publish in the city were prudentially Unionist.

Some Southerners, however, remained defiant. In the Confederate Congress on January 9, 1865, James W. Moore, a legislator from Kentucky, continued to insist that Sherman's march to the sea had been a failure. All that was needed now, he said, was legislation to fill up the Confederate armies. "It is true Sherman has Savannah," Moore said, "but with it he captured none of our troops. He left to us far more than he gained. . . . Our armies everywhere remain unbroken and invincible in spirit. Our material resources remain undiminished." Significantly no one in the House rose in support of Moore's statement. The tenor of the debate demonstrated that the Confederate lawmakers realized the damage that Sherman had done to the Confederate cause when his army had completed the march to the sea and captured Savannah. Southerners in Georgia understood this better than the Kentucky legislator. A number of Unionists asked Gov. Joe Brown to convene a special meeting to discuss the possibility of Georgia withdrawing from the war and suing for peace. Though nothing came of it, the fact that a separate peace was publicly discussed speaks volumes about the impact of Sherman's march to the sea.

10

THE FUTURE FOR FREED PEOPLE

As always seemed to be the case for Sherman in his tumultuous life, these good times did not last. He suffered a personal loss. As he began his march from Atlanta toward Savannah in mid-November, his family was busy in South Bend, Indiana, where several of his children were attending elementary school at what today are the University of Notre Dame and St. Mary's College. Ellen Sherman and the three youngest children, including three month old Charley, lived in a rented house owned by later vice president of the United States, Schuyler Colfax.

Baby Charley, whom Sherman had never seen, was suffering with the same asthma that had plagued his father all his life. As Sherman marched in Georgia, Charley grew worse in Indiana, and Ellen became increasingly upset. She had no contact with her husband who might be dead for all she knew, and their son was seriously ill. Their nine-year-old son Willy had died suddenly in the fall of 1863, and Ellen's mother had died in the spring of 1864, so death was fresh on her mind. On December 4, 1864, about the time that Sherman reached Millen, Georgia, two thirds of the way through the march, Charley succumbed to pneumonia. Ellen buried him on the Notre Dame campus, placing an artillery shell to mark his grave. Her husband, meanwhile, a thousand miles away, was dealing with land mines buried in the road toward Savannah.

Tragically, Ellen could not reach Sherman until December 30, so she suffered alone for most of that month. The Union general learned of his son's death before he heard it from Ellen, reading about it in the New York *Herald*. Although Willy's death devastated Sherman until the day he died, and his heart went out to Ellen at the death of Charley, he reacted passively to the demise of the child he had never seen. "I have seen death in such quantity and in such forms that it no longer startles me," he said. Ellen was more deeply affected and tied her feelings of loss to the success her husband had just achieved. Charley and Willy's deaths were "a lesson to us of the vanity of human glory," she warned Sherman.

Ellen Sherman, thus, grieved rather than celebrated her husband's momentous success, and several of Sherman's superiors also put another damper on his triumph. This time the problem concerned the slaves that accompanied his army, or had died in the effort to cross Ebenezer Creek. Sherman had a reputation for being anti-black, much of it the result of earlier statements opposing the arming of blacks and the sending of recruiters from northern states to enroll them.

In Washington, concern grew about the way Sherman was dealing with the mobs of refugees, the Ebenezer Creek episode providing, many thought, an enlightening insight into the general's beliefs. According to Henry Halleck, many people were convinced by the tragic incident at Ebenezer Creek that Sherman "manifested an almost *criminal* dislike to the Negro," whom Halleck called the "inevitable Sambo." Secretary of the Treasury Salmon P. Chase chimed in that Sherman should be aware that many important people believed that he "regard[ed] them [slaves] as a sort of pariah, almost without rights." And the statements in southern papers, allegedly coming from Sherman himself, that slavery would outlast the war and that he would own slaves himself, did not help his reputation. Nor did his letter to Halleck announcing the capture of Fort McAllister when he reported: "We have not lost a wagon on the trip, but have gathered in a large number of negroes, mules, horses, &c." His use of a black regiment in Savannah as a source for manual laborers also raised eyebrows. Army chaplain Henry M. Turner, a leading post-war black leader, best expressed Sherman's reputation when he came up with the phrase "*Shermanized* officers" to describe racist Union military leaders.

Sherman could not understand such criticism. He always insisted that he dealt properly with the black population; and beyond the usual white paternalism of the day, he did. Sherman related to everyone in the same way, with an open friendliness that made people immediately feel at home and sense his interest in them. He greeted former slaves in just that way, even shaking hands with them, an act that few whites as a whole and certainly fewer southern whites ever did. Black reaction to him ran the gauntlet from fervid excitement to calm acceptance. Many of his officers were taken aback at how familiar the general was with the black people he met, and how familiar they were with him. In Savannah, for example, when Sherman lived and worked in Charles Green's two story mansion, Henry Hitchcock said there was "a constant stream" of black people, "old and young, men, women and children, black, yellow, and cream-colored, uncouth and well-bred, bashful and talkative—but always respectful and behaved—all day long." Former slaves and freedmen felt very much at ease with the general; and he treated them respectfully, though, like many of his generation, he held a decidedly negative view of their capabilities.

Believing that his attitude toward the black population was appropriate, Sherman refused to accept warnings from Washington that he had an anti-black reputation. He told Halleck and Chase that his major concern was military, and not social. "But the nigger?" he thundered, "why, in God's name can't sensible men let him alone?" He had no problem with freedom for slaves, he said, though he could not imagine that it would be on terms of "equality with the Whites." This would result in a mixed race, and he believed such people had been the ruin of Mexico and South America. As for the idea of black suffrage, he believed that voting "should be rather abridged than enlarged." He understood that Chase, and others who wrote him on this subject, wanted him "to modify my opinions," he told Ellen, "but you know I cannot, for if I attempt the part of a hypocrite it would break out at each sentence. . . . I have said that slavery is dead and the Negro free, and want him treated as free, and not hunted and badgered to make a soldier of, when his family is left back on the plantations. I am right and won't change."

Secretary of War Edwin M. Stanton was not convinced. Sufficiently upset at reports of Sherman's alleged anti-black attitudes and actions, he decided to sail for Savannah to see for himself, arriving there on January 9, 1865. He and Sherman had several meetings and long talks. Stanton then had Sherman gather Savannah's black leaders, most of them ministers, to discuss their place in the new society. About twenty black men came to the gathering which took place in Sherman's room at the Green mansion. Stanton questioned the leaders about their understanding of recent events and asked for their advice on recruiting black soldiers and preparing for the post-emancipation world. Sherman found the whole episode puzzling, that the Secretary of War asked advice from black leaders.

Then Stanton asked Sherman to leave the room, and the general nearly lost his temper. But he waited outside while the Secretary of War asked the attendees: "State what is the feeling of the colored people toward General Sherman, and how far do they regard his sentiments and actions as friendly to their rights and interests or otherwise?' The black men expressed friendship toward Sherman. "His conduct and deportment toward us characterized him as a friend and gentleman," they said, "We have confidence in General Sherman, and think what concerns us could not be in better hands." Sherman was pleased when he learned about the statements, yet annoyed at Stanton for asking the question.

On January 16, 1865, Sherman issued one of the most significant documents to come out of the war, Special Field Orders No. 15. By its provisions, land, some thirty miles in from the ocean, from Charleston south, was set aside for the freed black population, with no white person, except for the military, "permitted to reside" there. Each black family would have the right to forty acres of land. Blacks could not be conscripted into the military service without presidential or congressional authority, but "young and able-bodied negroes must be encouraged to enlist as soldiers . . . to contribute their share toward maintaining their own freedom, and securing their rights as citizens of the United States."

This order could have been a revolutionary document and made a profound impact on the history of race relations in the reconstructed United States, had it been permanent. In fact, Sherman issued the document more to appease Stanton and as part of his psychological warfare against the white south, than as a way to aid the freed blacks. He never had any doubt that "the military authorities," meaning himself, "when war prevailed, had a perfect right to grant the possession of any vacant land to which they could extend military protection." But, he added significantly, the military could not and did not give "a fee-simple title." "All that was designed by these special field orders," he said, "was to make temporary provisions for the freed men and their families during the rest of the war, or until Congress should take action."

Sherman took no interest in implementing the orders, and once the war was over, President Andrew Johnson and his administration, and even the so-called Radical Republican Congress, refused to act. Johnson asked Sherman in 1866 for the reasoning behind the order, and when Sherman answered that he had always seen it as temporary and non-binding once the war ended, Johnson simply negated it. Significantly, Sherman never uttered a word in protest, though he was hardly as silent on numerous other Reconstruction matters. During these years, Sherman took a consistently pro-southern white position, agreeing with the attitude that, though slavery was dead, freed people should remain in a subservient position to the old-line white leadership. His march was instrumental in destroying slavery, but his reflection of nineteenth century prejudice against black people prevented him from accepting them as equal to whites. When the war was over, Sherman stood by his white southern friends as he had always promised he would once they laid down their arms.

11
SHERMAN'S FAME

Praise and congratulations poured in from every corner of the nation for the spectacular and undeniably successful completion of the march to the sea. Abraham Lincoln, Ulysses S. Grant, Henry W. Halleck, and Edwin M. Stanton, all of whom had doubted the wisdom of Sherman's plan before the Union army left Atlanta, now were effusive in their response to its successful conclusion. Lincoln, for example, admitted his prior anxiety and graciously concluded: "Now, the undertaking being a success, the honor is all yours." Halleck told Sherman that his march would "stand out prominently as the great one of this great war," while Grant called it a "most brilliant campaign." Stanton not only congratulated Sherman personally when he went to Savannah, but he also wrote Ellen Sherman: "Allow me to congratulate you upon the glorious consummation of your gallant husband's great operations against Savannah." On January 10, 1865, Congress passed a joint resolution "tendering the thanks of the people and of Congress to

Maj. Gen. William T. Sherman and the officers and soldiers of his command, for their gallant conduct in their late brilliant movement through Georgia."

Citizens of all description joined in the praise, as did officials on the state level. One of Sherman's former West Point professors, the famous Dennis Hart Mahan, was excited about his former student's "splendid success," while businessman George Templeton Strong called "Sherman's grand adagio movement through Georgia . . . among the best and boldest conceptions of the war and . . . the most triumphantly executed." Magazine editor and critic E.L. Godkin called Sherman a "real genius." Frederick F. Low, the governor of California, thanked Sherman, a great leader, . . . for the signal services your army has rendered to the cause of civilization, liberty, humanity, and good government." The New York state legislature, meanwhile, complimented Sherman and his men "for the series of superb victories . . . which challenged the admiration of the world . . . and demonstrated that the so-called Confederacy is indeed but a 'shell.'" Even the mayor and city council of Savannah praised Sherman for his successful organization of the northern relief effort for the city after its capture.

The press joined the volume of congratulations sounding across the land. Even before Sherman arrived on the coast, the Washington *Chronicle*, responding to Confederate predictions of disaster for the marching Union army, told its readers that "whatever Sherman may attempt he will probably succeed in accomplishing." A reporter who had somehow traveled with the army indicated just how much press attitudes toward the general had changed. Where the typical newspaper view of Sherman had always been almost uniformly negative, now New York *Herald* correspondent John E. Hayes told his editor that "Gen'l Sherman is an earnest, honest, truly loyal man, and the more I see and hear of him, the stronger grows my attachment and admiration for the man." The New York *Tribune* said that

"Savannah is fallen like a ripe apple into Sherman's lap. . . . And the truth is, Gen. Sherman may go where he chooses and do what he pleases." And the Chicago *Tribune* went even further. It called him "our Military Santa Claus" and concluded that "Sherman's march [has] a place parallel with the Anabasis and the best efforts of Marlborough, Napoleon, and Wellington."

The British were equally full of praise. The *London Times* also likened Sherman to Marlborough and Napoleon. The *British Army and Navy Gazette* said that it was clear "that, so long as he roams about with his army inside the Confederate States, he is more deadly than twenty Grants, and that he must be destroyed if Richmond or any thing is to be saved." The *London Herald* saw his success as allowing "his name . . . [to be] written on the tablet of fame, side by side with that of Napoleon and Hannibal."

This verbal outpouring also took concrete form. Even before Sherman reached the sea, U.S. Grant and business leaders in Cincinnati, independently of each other, began a subscription campaign to build a house for the Shermans in that Ohio city, Grant pledging $500. Although the Shermans never lived in Cincinnati, this fund drive and others like it resulted in the family later receiving a house in Washington and a substantial sum of money besides.

At the same time that people were raising money as a way of congratulating Sherman on his successful military campaign, others were recommending him for promotion in rank. Sherman reacted negatively to the idea. On January 19, 1865, he wrote his senator brother, John: "I don't want Promotion. . . . The Law cannot confer Military fame, nor can it make my right to command greater than it now is. I have all the Power that can possibly be exercised. Acts of special Legislation never do good. When the War is over there will be time enough for honors and Provisions, but now every positive pretext for jealousy and envy should be avoided." Just three days later, Sherman made his reasoning even clearer, demonstrating his complete loyalty to Grant, "I will accept no commission that would tend to create a rivalry with Grant. I want him to hold what he has earned and got. I have all the rank I want." As for the suggestion that he seek political office, he told his brother to tell anyone who brought up that idea that he "would be offended by such association."

Most significantly to him, Sherman enjoyed the cheers and affection of his soldiers. W.G. Shotwell expressed it clearly. The march to the sea "was the most halcyon period in their service and one to which in after years their minds oftenest reverted with joyful recollection." There were no charges against entrenchments leading to horrendous death and maiming, and no huge armies were there to battle. Sherman's men saw themselves winning the war at the least risk to life and limb, and they appreciated the general who made it possible for them.

Having reached the pinnacle of public and private satisfaction, Sherman was in a fine mood. "I have received from high sources highest praise[,] and yesterday, New Year, was toasted, etc., with allusions to Hannibal, Caesar, etc. etc.," he told Ellen. "But in reply I turned all into a good joke by saying that Hannibal and Caesar were small potatoes as they had never read the New York *Herald*, or had a photograph taken. But of course, I feel a just pride in the confidence of my army, and the singular friendship of General Grant." But it was all still hard to believe. "Like one who has walked a narrow plank, I look back and wonder if I really did it," he confided to Ellen.

Sherman really was proud of his achievement and, as might be expected, he expressed it best to his army. He issued Special Field Orders No. 6 on January 8, 1865, thanking his soldiers for all that they had done together in Georgia and at the battle of Nashville in Tennessee, "So complete a success in military operations extending over a half a continent is an achievement that entitles it (the army) to a place in the military history of the world." And in later years, Sherman never changed his mind. He told his youngest son that "General Lee had committed a grave error in letting him get through without making a concerted effort to crush his army."

Sherman was not finished marching through the Confederacy when the Union army reached Savannah. The early months of 1865 saw him replicate his march to the sea by marching through the Carolinas. Meanwhile, Phil Sheridan had already eliminated Jubal Early's army in the Shenandoah Valley and had devastated the land in a manner more destructive than Sherman. Grant kept hammering away at Lee, pinning him down and inexorably wearing down the Army of Northern Virginia. In April, Lee surrendered to Grant, and within days, Confederate Gen. Joseph E. Johnston surrendered to Sherman, receiving from him such generous terms that Washington had to impose stricter provisions. The war thus came to an end, and Sherman's march to the sea had played an important role in speeding its completion. And when the hard war ended, as Sherman had promised, he offered the softest peace possible.

Sherman's object in marching through Georgia, after all, was to end the war as quickly as possible with the least loss of life so the nation could return to its prewar relationships. Recognizing that warfare was between societies and not merely between armies in the field, the general believed that, even if the Union army defeated the Confederate army, the war would still go on if southern society maintained its will to continue resistance. Sherman determined to bring the war home to civilian society, to demoralize it psychologically, and convince it to stop supporting the Confederate armies.

To the average twenty-first century American, Sherman is the father of "total war," the kind of conflict that devastated the world during the twentieth century. One author even saw Sherman's historical hand in the kind of fighting that took place in Viet Nam. Historians, in fact, debate the meaning of the term "total war," disagreeing about characterizing what Sherman did during his marches with that term. Sherman never completely erased the barrier that existed between the civilian and the soldier, although he did bring the war home to southern society in a dramatic fashion. But, Sherman was never a total warrior. He emphasized limited destruction for a specific purpose: to end the war as quickly as possible. This was not a total approach. In the Federal army's march to the sea there were no unforgiving assaults on civilians; no solid swath of destruction sixty miles wide and 300 miles long. Sherman never even had any thought of forcing the Confederacy to adhere completely to Union demands before he would stop the destruction. He took the opposite position. Once the southern armies quit fighting, he would welcome Southerners back into the Union with all the rights and privileges they had enjoyed before the war's beginning. Sherman supported a *status quo ante bellum* end to the conflict. He opposed any enforced wholesale changes in southern society; Sherman simply wanted the war to end, and the Union restored as it had once been, slavery and all.

Historian Mark Neely was right when he called Sherman "a nineteenth century soldier at work." In his march to the sea, as this book has demonstrated, Sherman did not wage modern total war against his enemy. He destroyed in order to make the war less total, less maiming, less life threatening. He did not try to destroy opposing armies that faced him, demonstrating what some historians have identified as the lack of a killer instinct. He did not want to kill enemy soldiers; he wanted to convince them to stop fighting and become friends again in a reestablished Union. Sherman's contribution to the strategy of war was purposeful destruction to save lives, not total war to smash the opposition. In modern war, military strategists use destruction to try to save their own soldiers' and civilians' lives. The bombing they employ to do this inevitably kills and maims enemy soldiers and civilians. Sherman well understood the theory of destructive war as he waged it, but he would find the modern execution appalling.

Sherman's Civil War destruction did not immediately convince Confederate soldiers and civilians that they were doomed, however. As long as Lee was in the field, many Southerners unrealistically continued to hope that somehow their side would win. Historian George Rable put it this way: "Rationalization and wishful thinking helped citizens hang onto hope even in the absence of any tangible reasons to do so." There was, Rable said, "a reluctance to face reality." Sherman was an essential part of that reality, however, and he helped make such denial difficult to continue for very long.

In February 1865, Robert E. Lee bemoaned "the state of despondency" among southern civilians and its consequent influence on the increased desertions in his army, while Jefferson Davis expressed concern about Sherman's campaign's "bad effect on our people. Success against his future operations," Davis warned, "is needed to reanimate public confidence." The soldier reaction grew increasingly desperate. One Confederate soldier stated, "I don't like this way of fighting here in Virginia and letting the Yankees run all over Georgia. I had rather fight for those that I love." Another common Confederate soldier, however, expressed it better, if not completely accurately, after the war, "As soon as I saw the lines of his fire I said confidentially to my captain, 'Our men in Virginia can't stand this. Sherman has whipped us with fire. He drives the women and children out of Atlanta and then burns the country ahead of them. Our cause is lost.' And it was." Some Confederate men and women no doubt maintained their animosity, but many others lost the desire to continue the fight and urged their soldiers to return and save them.

When that Confederate soldier said: "Our cause is lost," he could not realize that what came to be called the "Lost Cause" would live on as part of the conventional view of Civil War history. And the former Confederate soldier could not know that

William T. Sherman, the victor of the march to the sea, would suffer that campaign's greatest loss in the eyes of history. In the twentieth century, despite his contribution to military history, Sherman's reputation became not that of a purposeful destroyer but of an unfeeling, uncaring sadistic brute. He was *the* villain of a hard war. Historian Victor Davis Hanson concluded: "In short, the South despised Sherman not because he had defeated them, but because he had humiliated them in the process." Historian Paul Buck said that "Sherman personified all that the South had suffered." His destruction of property was viewed as worse than the killing and maiming of soldiers in pitched battles between Grant and Lee. Sherman was accused of marching and destroying in areas where he never visited, and the general was held responsible for devastation the Union army never did. Conversely, a variety of towns he bypassed or left essentially unharmed have legends surrounding them attributing their survival to women momentarily civilizing the brutish invader. What actually happened, as historian Anne Bailey phrased it, that "he had helped reunite the country," has been lost somewhere in the shadowy mists of myth.

Sherman's own soldiers, however, never had any doubt of the importance of what the Union army had done in Georgia. Indiana soldier William Bluffton Miller insisted in a later pension letter that he had helped "the sun of the Confederacy" set into "everlasting night." Ironically, modern folklorist Elissa R. Henken has discovered that Georgia remembrances are just the opposite, "The South may have lost the war, but it was never defeated; the town and its womenfolk [in preventing destruction] conquered the conqueror." The cause was not lost. The psychological battle that Sherman inaugurated in 1864 continues in the twenty-first century.

APPENDIX A

Sherman's fame was cemented in history after finishing his march to the sea. Many songs and plays were written about the general and his exploits soon after word of Sherman's success reached the North. Below are some illustrations from those works.

DEDICATED TO THE VETERANS OF SHERMAN'S ARMY.

THE MARCHING SONG OF SHERMAN'S ARMY.

SHERMAN

MARCHED DOWN TO THE SEA.

A Patriotic Refrain.

WORDS BY ADJ'T BYERS.

Music by

W. C. PETERS.

PIANO.

3⅜

GUITAR.

Published.

Cincinnati: A. C. PETERS & BRO: — J. L. PETERS & BRO: St. Louis.

3990

Text of a poem by S.H.M. Byers, written by this Union officer while in a Confederate prison and given to Sherman in Columbia, South Carolina, in early February 1865, later put to music, and widely published and performed.

SHERMAN'S MARCH TO THE SEA.   67

Our camp-fire shone bright on the mountains
  That frowned on the river below,
While we stood by our guns in the morning,
  And eagerly watched for the foe;
When a rider came out from the darkness
  That hung over mountain and tree,
And shouted, " Boys, up and be ready,
  For Sherman will march to the sea."

Then cheer upon cheer for bold Sherman,
  Went up from each valley and glen,
And the bugles rechoed the music,
  That came from the lips of the men.
For we knew that the stars on our banner
  More bright in their splendor would be,
And that blessings from Northland wou'' greet us
  When Sherman marched down to the sea.

Then forward, boys, forward to battle,
  We marched on our wearisome way,
And we stormed the wild hills of Resaca,
  God bless those who fell on that day!
Then Kenesaw, dark in its glory,
  Frowned down on the flag of the free,
But the East and the West bore our standards,
  And Sherman marched down to the sea.

Still onward we pressed till our banners
  Swept out from Atlanta's grim walls,
And the blood of the patriot dampened
  The soil where the traitor's flag falls;
But we paused not to weep for the fallen,
  Who slept by each river and tree,
Yet we twined them a wreath of the laurel,
  As Sherman marched down to the sea.

Oh, proud was our army that morning,
  That stood where the pine proudly towers,
When Sherman said, " Boys, you are weary,
  This day fair Savannah is ours!"
Then sung we a song for our chieftain,
  That echoed o'er river and lea,
And the stars in our banner shone brighter,
  When Sherman marched down to the sea.

And now, though our marching is over,
  And peace and the Union are sure,
We think we will finish our labor,
  And all that we fought for secure
By voting for wise men and true men
  That they may our sentinels be,
To guard what our gallant men went for
  When Sherman marched down to the sea.

Words of the very popular musical composition "Marching Through Georgia," written by Henry Clay Work in 1865 and, next to the "Battle Hymn of the Republic," probably the most popular song to come out of the Civil War. The South, then and in later years, considered it provocative.

MARCHING THROUGH GEORGIA. 113

By permission of ROOT and CADY.

Bring the good old bugle, boys! we'll sing another song—
Sing it with that spirit that will start the world along—
Sing it as we used to sing it fifty thousand strong,
 While we were marching through Georgia.

CHORUS.

"Hurrah! hurrah! we bring the Jubilee!
Hurrah! Hurrah! the flag that makes you free!"
So we sing the chorus from Atlanta to the sea,
 While we were marching through Georgia.

How the darkies shouted when they heard the joyful sound!
How the turkeys gobbled which our commissary found!
How the sweet potatoes even started from the ground,
 While we were marching through Georgia.
      Hurrah, hurrah! &c.

Yes, and there were Union men who wept with joyful tears,
When they saw the honored flag they had not seen for years;
Hardly could they be restrained from breaking off in cheers,
 While we were marching through Georgia.
      Hurrah, hurrah! &c.

"Sherman's dashing Yankee boys will never reach the coast!"
So the saucy rebels said, and 'twas a handsome boast,
Had they not forgot, alas, to reckon with the host,
 While we marching through Georgia.
      Hurrah, hurrah! &c.

So we made a thoroughfare for Freedom and her train,
Sixty miles in latitude—three hundred to the main;
Treason fled before us, for resistance was in vain,
 While we were marching through Georgia.
      Hurrah, hurrah! &c.

But the march is not yet finished, nor will we yet disband,
While still a trace of treason remains to curse the land,
Or any foe against the flag uplifts a threatening hand,
 For we've been marching through Georgia.
      Hurrah, hurrah! &c.

When Right is in the White House and Wisdom in her seat
The reconstructed Senators and Congress men to greet,
Why then we may stop marching, and rest our weary feet,
 For we've been marching through Georgia.
      Hurrah, hurrah! &c.

APPENDIX B

Organization of the Union Forces, commanded by Maj. Gen. William T. Sherman

HEADQUARTERS GUARD

7th Company Ohio Sharpshooters, Lieut. James Cox

ENGINEERS
1st Missouri (five companies), Lieut. Col. William Tweeddale

RIGHT WING
Maj. Gen. OLIVER O. HOWARD

ESCORT
15th Illinois Cavalry, Company K, Lieut. John A. McQueen
4th Company Ohio Cavalry, Capt. John L. King

FIFTEENTH ARMY CORPS
Maj. Gen. PETER J. OSTERHAUS

FIRST DIVISION
Brig. Gen. CHARLES R. WOODS

First Brigade
Col. MILO SMITH

12th Indiana, Maj. Elbert D. Baldwin
26th Iowa, Maj. John Lubbers
27th Missouri, Col. Thomas Curly
29th Missouri, Lieut. Col. Joseph S. Gage

31st and 32d Missouri Battalion, Maj. Abraham J. Seay
76th Ohio, Col. William B. Woods

Second Brigade
Brig. Gen. CHARLES C. WALCUTT*
Col. ROBERT F. CATTERSON

26th Illinois, Capt. George H. Reed
40th Illinois, Lieut. Col. Hiram W. Hall
103d Illinois, Maj. Aslas Willison
97th Indiana:
Col. Robert F. Catterson
Capt. George Elliott
100th Indiana, Maj. Ruel M. Johnson
6th Iowa, Maj. William H. Clune
46th Ohio, Lieut. Col. Isaac N. Alexander

Third Brigade
Col. JAMES A. WLLIAMSON

4th Iowa, Lieut. Col. Samuel D. Nichols
9th Iowa, Capt. Paul McSweeney
25th Iowa, Col. George A. Stone
30th Iowa, Lieut. Col. Aurelius Roberts
31st Iowa, Lieut. Col. Jeremiah W. Jenkins

SECOND DIVISION
Brig. Gen. WILLIAM B. HAZEN

First Brigade
Col. THEODORE JONES

55th Illinois, Capt. Charles A. Andreas
116th Illinois, Lieut. Col. John E. Maddux
127th Illinois, Capt. Charles Schryver
6th Missouri, Lieut. Col. Delos Van Deusen
6th Missouri (two companies), Capt. John W. White
30th Ohio, Capt. Emory W. Muenscher
57th Ohio, Maj. John McClure

Second Brigade
Col. WELLS S. JONES+
Col. JAMES S. MARTIN

111th Illinois:
Col. James S. Martin
Maj. William M. Mabry
83d Indiana, Lieut. Col. George H. Scott
37th Ohio, Lieut. Col. Louis von Blessingh
47th Ohio, Col. Augustus C. Parry
53d Ohio, Capt. David H. Lasley
54th Ohio, Lieut. Col. Israel T. Moore

* Wounded November 22
+ Wounded December 13

Third Brigade
Col. JOHN M. OLIVER

48th Illinois, Maj. Edward Adams
90th Illinois, Lieut. Col. Owen Stuart
99th Indiana, Lieut. Col. John M. Berkey
15th Michigan, Lieut. Col. Frederick S. Hutchinson
70th Ohio, Lieut. Col. Henry L. Philips

THIRD DIVISION
Brig. Gen. JOHN E. SMITH

First Brigade
Col. JOSEPH B. McCOWN

63d Illinois, Lieut. Col. James Isaminger
93d Illinois,* Lieut. Col. Nicholas C. Buswell
48th Indiana, Lieut. Col. Edward J. Wood
59th Indiana, Lieut. Col. Jefferson K. Scott
4th Minnesota, Col. John E. Tourtellotte

Second Brigade
Bvt. Brig. Gen. GREEN B. RAUM

56th Illinois, Capt. James P. Files
10th Iowa, Lieut. Col. Paris P. Henderson
26th Missouri,+ Col. Benjamin D. Dean
80th Ohio, Lieut. Col. Pren Metham

FOURTH DIVISION
Brig. Gen. JOHN M. CORSE

First Brigade
Brig. Gen. ELLIOTT W. RICE

52d Illinois:
Maj. Wesley Boyd
Lieut. Col. Jerome D. Davis
66th Indiana, Lieut. Col. Roger Martin
2d Iowa, Lieut. Col. Noel B. Howard
7th Iowa, Lieut. Col. James C. Parrott

Second Brigade
Col. ROBERT N. ADAMS

12th Illinois, Lieut. Col. Henry Van Sellar
66th Illinois, Lieut. Col. Andrew K. Campbell
81st Ohio, Maj. William C. Henry

*Non-veterans 18th Wisconsin attached
+Detachment 10th Missouri attached

Third Brigade
Lieut. Col. FREDERICK J. HURLBUT

7th Illinois, Lieut. Col. Hector Perrin
50th Illinois, Capt. Henry Horn
57th Illinois, Capt. Frederick A. Battey
39th Iowa, Maj. Joseph M. Griffiths

ARTILLERY
Maj. CHARLES J. STOLBRAND

1st Illinois Light, Battery H, Capt. Francis De Gress
1st Michigan Light, Battery B, Capt. Albert F.R. Arndt
1st Missouri Light, Battery H, Lieut. John F. Brunner
Wisconsin Light, 12th Battery, Capt. William Zickerick

SEVENTEENTH ARMY CORPS
Maj. Gen. FRANK P. BLAIR, JR.

ESCORT
11th Illinois Cavalry, Company G, Capt. Stephen S. Tripp

FIRST DIVISION
Maj. Gen. JOSEPH A. MOWER

First Brigade
Brig. Gen. JOHN W. FULLER

64th Illinois, Capt. Joseph S. Reynolds
18th Missouri, Lieut. Col. Charles S. Sheldon
27th Ohio, Capt. James Morgan
39th Ohio, Capt. Daniel Weber

Second Brigade
Brig. Gen. JOHN W. SPRAGUE

35th New Jersey, Col. John J. Cladek
43d Ohio, Col. Wager Swayne
63d Ohio, Maj. John W. Fouis
25th Wisconsin, Lieut. Col. Jeremiah M. Rusk

Third Brigade
Col. JOHN TILLSON

10th Illinois, Lieut. Col. McLain F. Wood
25th Indiana, Maj. James S. Wright
32d Wisconsin, Col. Charles H. De Groat

THIRD DIVISION
Brig. Gen. MORTIMER D. LEGGETT

Provost Guard
20th Illinois, Capt. Henry King

First Brigade
Brig. Gen. MANNING F. FORCE

30th Illinois, Lieut. Col. William C. Rhoads
31st Illinois, Lieut. Col. Robert N. Pearson
45th Illinois, Maj. John O. Duer
12th Wisconsin, Lieut. Col. James K. Proudfit
16th Wisconsin, Maj. William F. Dawes

Second Brigade
Col. ROBERT K. SCOTT

20th Ohio, Capt. Lyman N. Ayres
68th Ohio, Lieut. Col. George E. Welles
78th Ohio, Col. Greenberry F. Wiles
17th Wisconsin, Maj. Patrick H. McCauley

FOURTH DIVISION
Brig. Gen. GILES A. SMITH

First Brigade
Col. BENJAMIN F. POTTS

14th Illinois} (battalion), Lieut. Alonzo J. Gillespie
15th Illinois} (battalion), Lieut. Alonzo J. Gillespie
41st Illinois (battalion), Maj. Robert H. McFadden
53d Illinois, Col. John W. McClanahan
23d Indiana, Lieut. Col. George S. Babbitt
53d Indiana, Capt. Henry Duncan
32d Ohio, Lieut. Col. Jefferson J. Hibbets

Third Brigade
Brig. Gen. WILLIAM W. BELKNAP

32d Illinois, Maj. Henry Davidson
11th Iowa, Capt. Benjamin Beach
13th Iowa, Capt. Justin C. Kennedy
15th Iowa, Maj. George Pomutz
16th Iowa, Capt. Crandall W. Williams

ARTILLERY
Maj. ALLEN C. WATERHOUSE

1st Michigan Light, Battery C, Lieut. Henry Shier
Minnesota Light, 1st Battery, Lieut. Henry Hurter
Ohio Light, 15th Battery, Lieut. George R. Caspar

LEFT WING
Maj. Gen. HENRY W. SLOCUM

PONTONIERS
58th Indiana, Col. George P. Buell

ENGINEERS
1st Michigan (detachment), Maj. John B. Yates

FOURTEENTH ARMY CORPS
Bvt. Maj. Gen. JEFFERSON C. DAVIS

FIRST DIVISION
Brig. Gen. WILIAM P. CARLIN

First Brigade
Col. HARRISON C. HOBART

104th Illinois, Lieut. Col. Douglas Hapeman
42d Indiana, Capt. Gideon R. Kellams
88th Indiana, Lieut. Col. Cyrus E. Briant
33d Ohio, Capt. Joseph Hinson
94th Ohio, Lieut. Col. Rue P. Hutchins
21st Wisconsin, Lieut. Col. Michael H. Fitch

Second Brigade
Lieut. Col. JOSEPH H. BRIGHAM

13th Michigan, Lieut. Col. Theodoric R. Palmer
21st Michigan, Maj. Benton D. Fox
69th Ohio, Capt. Lewis E. Hicks

Third Brigade
Col. HENRY A. HAMBRIGHT*
Lieut. Col. DAVID MILES

38th Indiana, Capt. James H. Low
21st Ohio, Lieut. Col. Arnold McMahan
74th Ohio:
Maj. Joseph Fisher
Maj. Robert P. Findley
79th Pennsylvania:
Lieut. Col. David Miles
Maj. Michael H. Locher

* Sick from November 18

SECOND DIVISION
Brig. Gen. JAMES D. MORGAN

First Brigade
Col. ROBERT F. SMITH

16 Illinois, Lieut. Col. James B. Cahill
60th Illinois, Col. William B. Anderson
10th Michigan, Col. Charles M. Lum
14th Michigan, Maj. Thomas C. Fitzgibbon
17th New York, Lieut. Col. Joel O. Martin

Second Brigade
Lieut. Col. JOHN S. PEARCE

34th Illinois, Capt. Peter Ege
78th Illinois, Lieut. Col. Maris R. Vernon
98th Ohio, Capt. James R. McLaughlin
108th Ohio, Maj. Frederick Beck
113th Ohio, Capt. Toland Jones
121st Ohio, Maj. Aaron B. Robinson

Third Brigade
Lieut. Col. JAMES W. LANGLEY

85th Illinois, Maj. Robert G. Rider
86th Illinois, Lieut. Col. Allen L. Fahnestock
110th Illinois (four companies), Lieut. Col. E. Hibbard Topping
125th Illinois, Capt. George W. Cook
22d Indiana, Capt. William H. Snodgrass
52d Ohio, Lieut. Col. Charles W. Clancy

THIRD DIVISION
Brig. Gen. ABSALOM BAIRD

First Brigade
Col. MORTON C. HUNTER

82d Indiana, Lieut. Col. John M. Matheny
23d Missouri, Lieut. Col. Quin Morton
17th Ohio, Lieut. Col. Benjamin H. Showers
31st Ohio, Capt. Michael Stone
89th Ohio, Lieut. Col. William H. Glenn
92d Ohio,* Col. Benjamin D. Fearing

Second Brigade
Col. NEWELL GLEASON

75th Indiana, Maj. Cyrus J. McCole
87th Indiana, Lieut. Col. Edwin P. Hammond
101st Indiana, Lieut. Col. Thomas Doan
2d Minnesota, Lieut. Col. Judson W. Bishop
105th Ohio, Lieut. Col. George T. Perkins

* Company A; 24th Illinois attached.

Third Brigade
Col. GEORGE P. ESTE

74th Indiana, Lieut. Col. Thomas Morgan
18th Kentucky, Lieut. Col. Hubbard K. Milward
14th Ohio, Lieut. Col Albert Moore
38th Ohio, Capt. Charles M. Gilbert

ARTILLERY
Maj. CHARLES HOUGHTALING

1st Illinois Light, Battery C,+ Lieut. Joseph R. Channel
2d Illinois Light, Battery I, Lieut. Alonzo W. Coe
Indiana Light, 19th Battery, Capt. William P. Stackhouse
Wisconsin Light, 5th Battery, Lieut. Joseph McKnight

TWENTIETH ARMY CORPS
Brig. Gen. ALPHEUS S. WILLIAMS

FIRST DIVISION
Brig. Gen. NATHANIEL J. JACKSON

First Brigade
Col. JAMES L. SELFRIDGE

5th Connecticut, Lieut. Col. Henry W. Daboll
123d New York, Lieut. Col. James C. Rogers
141st New York, Capt. William Merrell
46th Pennsylvania, Maj. Patrick Griffith

Second Brigade
Col. EZRA A. CARMAN

2d Massachusetts, Col. William Cogswell
13th New Jersey, Maj. Frederick H. Harris
107th New York:
Capt. Charles J. Fox
Lieut. Col. Allen N. Sill
150th New York:
Maj. Alfred B. Smith
Col. John H. Ketcham
3d Wisconsin, Col. William Hawley

Third Brigade
Col. JAMES S. ROBINSON

82d Illinois, Maj. Ferdinand H. Rolshausen
101st Illinois, Lieut. Col. John B. Le Sage
143d New York, Lieut. Col. Hezekiah Watkins
61st Ohio, Capt. John Garrett
82d Ohio, Lieut. Col. David Thomson
31st Wisconsin, Col. Francis H. West

+ Detachment 11th Ohio Infantry attached.

SECOND DIVISION
Brig. Gen. JOHN W. GEARY

First Brigade
Col. ARIO PARDEE, JR.

5th Ohio, Lieut. Col. Robert Kirkup
29th Ohio:
Maj. Myron T. Wright*
Capt. Jonas Schoonover
66th Ohio, Lieut. Col. Eugene Powell
28th Pennsylvania, Col. John Flynn
147th Pennsylvania,+ Lieut. Col. John Craig

Second Brigade
Col. PATRICK H. JONES

33d New Jersey, Col. George W. Mindil
119th New York, Col. John T. Lockman
134th New York, Lieut. Col. Allan H. Jackson
154th New York, Maj. Lewis D. Warner
73d Pennsylvania, Maj. Charles C. Cresson
109th Pennsylvania, Capt. Walter G. Dunn

Third Brigade
Col. HENRY A. BARNUM

60th New York, Maj. Thomas Elliott
102d New York, Lieut. Col. Harvey S. Chatfield
137th New York, Lieut. Col. Koert S. Van Voorhis
149th New York, Maj. Nicholas Grumbach
29th Pennsylvania, Lieut. Col. Samuel M. Zulich
111th Pennsylvania, Lieut. Col. Thomas M. Walker

THIRD DIVISION
Brig. Gen. WILLIAM T. WARD

First Brigade
Col. FRANKLIN C. SMITH

102d Illinois, Maj. Hiland H. Clay
105th Illinois, Maj. Henry D. Brown
129th Illinois, Col. Henry Case
70th Indiana, Lieut. Col. Samuel Merrill
79th Ohio, Lieut. Col. Azariah W. Doan

Second Brigade
Col. DANIEL DUSTIN

33d Indiana, Lieut. Col. James E. Burton
85th Indiana, Lieut. Col. Alexander B. Crane
19th Michigan, Lieut. Col. John J. Baker
22d Wisconsin, Lieut. Col. Edward Bloodgood

* Wounded December 19.
+ Detachment Battery E, Pennsylvania Artillery, attached.

Third Brigade
Col. SAMUEL ROSS

20th Connecticut, Lieut. Col. Philo B. Buckingham
33d Massachusetts, Lieut. Col. Elisha Doane
136th New York, Lieut. Col. Lester B. Faulkner
55th Ohio, Lieut. Col. Edwin H. Powers
73d Ohio, Lieut. Col. Samuel H. Hurst
26th Wisconsin, Lieut. Col. Frederick C. Winkler

ARTILLERY
Maj. JOHN A. REYNOLDS

1st New York Light, Battery I, Capt. Charles E. Winegar
1st New York Light, Battery M, Lieut. Edward P. Newkirk
1st Ohio Light, Battery C, Capt. Marco B. Gary,[1] Lieut. Jerome B. Stephens
Pennsylvania Light, Battery E, Capt. Thomas S. Sloan

CAVALRY

THIRD DIVISION
Brig. Gen. JUDSON KILPATRICK

First Brigade
Col. ELI H. MURRAY

8th Indiana, Lieut. Col. Fielder A. Jones
2d Kentucky:
Capt. Joseph T. Forman
Capt. Robert M. Gilmore
3d Kentucky, Lieut. Col. Robert H. King
5th Kentucky, Col. Oliver L. Baldwin
9th Pennsylvania, Col. Thomas J. Jordan

Second Brigade
Col. SMITH D. ATKINS

92d Illinois (mounted infantry), Lieut. Col. Matthew Van Buskirk
3d Indiana, Capt. Charles U. Patton
9th Michigan, Col. George S. Acker
5th Ohio, Col. Thomas T. Heath
9th Ohio, Col. William D. Hamilton
10th Ohio, Lieut. Col. Thomas W. Sanderson
McLaughlin's (Ohio) Squadron, Capt. John Dalzell

Unattached
1st Alabama Cavalry,[2] Col. George E. Spencer
9th Illinois Mounted Infantry,[3] Lieut. Col. Samuel T. Hughes

[1] Captured December 12.
[2] Serving with the Left Wing.
[3] From returns of the commands indicated.

Artillery
10th Wisconsin Battery, Capt. Yates V. Beebe

Commanded by Maj. Gen. Oliver O. Howard
Commanded by Maj. Gen. Peter J. Osterhaus

FURTHER READING

Bailey, Anne J. *The Chessboard of War, Sherman and Hood in the Autumn Campaigns of 1864.* Lincoln: University of Nebraska Press, 2000.

_____. *War and Ruin, William T. Sherman and the Savannah Campaign.* Wilmington, Delaware: Scholarly Resources, 2003.

Bohrnstedt, Jennifer Cain, ed. *Soldiering with Sherman, the Civil War Letters of George J. Cram.* Dekalb, Illinois: Northern Illinois University Press, 2000.

Bragg, Willliam Harris. *Griswoldville.* Macon: Mercer University Press, 2000.

Brockett, L.P., *Men of Our Day. . . .* St. Louis: Zeigler, McCurdy, 1868.

Burne, Alfred H. *Lee, Grant and Sherman, A Study in Leadership in the 1864-65 Campaign.* Aldershot: Gale and Polden, 1938, reprinted in paperback by University of Kansas Press, 2000.

Byers, S.H.M. *With Fire and Sword.* New York: Neale, 1911.

Campbell, Jacqueline Glass. *When Sherman Marched North From the the Sea, Resistance on the Confederate Home Front.* Chapel Hill: University of North Carolina Press, 1999.

Carlin, William Passmore. *The Memoirs of Brigadier General William Passmore Carlin, U.S.A.* ed. by Robert I. Girardi and Nathaniel Cheairs Hughes, Jr. Lincoln: University of Nebraska Press, 1999.

Carpenter, John A. *Sword and Olive Branch: Oliver Otis Howard.* Pittsburgh: University of Pittsburgh Press, 1964.

Castel, Albert. *Tom Taylor's Civil War.* Lawrence: University Press of Kansas, 2000.

Cashin, Edward J. *General Sherman's Great Fraud and Other Stories about Augusta.* Spartanburg, S.C.: The Reprint Co. for Woodstone Press, 1994.

Conyngham, David P. *Sherman's March Through the South with Sketches and Incidents of the Campaign.* New York: Sheldon, 1865.

Cox, Jacob D. *The March to the Sea: Franklin and Nashville.* Vol. 10 in Scribner's Campaigns of the Civil War series. New York: Charles Scribner's Sons, 1882.

Davis, Burke. *Sherman's March.* New York: Random House, 1980.

DeLaubenfels, D.J. "Where Sherman Passed By," *Geographical Review* 47 (1957): 381-95.

_____. "With Sherman Through Georgia," *Georgia Historical Quarterly* 41 (1957): 288-300.

Donald, David Herbert. *Lincoln.* New York: Simon and Schuster, 1995.

Drago, Edmund L. "How Sherman's March Through Georgia Affected The Slaves," *Georgia Historical Quarterly* 57 (Autumn 1973): 361-75.

Dyer, John P. *"Fighting Joe" Wheeler.* Baton Rouge: Louisiana State University Press, 1941.

Fellman, Michael. *Citizen Sherman: A Life of William Tecumseh Sherman.* New York: Random House, 1995.

Foote, Corydon Edward, with Olive Deane Hormel. *With Sketches to the Sea, A Drummer's Story of the Civil War.* New York: John Day, 1960.

Foster, Buckley Thomas. "Dress Rehearsal for Hard War: William T. Sherman and the Meridian Campaign," Ph.D. diss., Mississippi State University, 2003.

Frank, Lisa Tendrich. "To 'Cure Her of Her Pride and Boasting': The Gendered Implications of Sherman's March," Ph.D. diss., University of Florida, 2002.

Glatthaar, Joseph T. *Forged in Battle: the Civil War Alliance of Black Soldiers and White Officers*. New York: The Free Press, 1990.

_____. *The March to the Sea and Beyond: Sherman's Troops in the Savannah and Carolina Campaigns*. New York: New York University Press, 1985.

Grant, Ulysses S. *Personal Memoirs of U.S. Grant*. 2 vols. New York: Charles L. Webster, 1885-1886.

Gray, Tom S., Jr. "The March to the Sea," *Georgia Historical Quarterly* 14 (1930): 111-38.

Grimsley, Mark. *The Hard Hand of War, Union Military Policy Toward Southern Civilians 1861-1865*. New York: Cambridge University Press, 1995.

_____ and Brooks D. Simpson, eds. *The Collapse of the Confederacy, Key Issues of the Civil War* (essays by Jean V. Berlin, William B. Feis, Mark Grimsley, George C. Rable, Brooks D. Simpson, Steven E. Woodworth) Lincoln: University of Nebraska Press, 2001.

Hanson, Victor Davis. *The Soul of Battle, From Ancient Times to Present Day, How Three Great Liberators Vanquished Tyranny*. New York: The Free Press, 1999.

Harwell, Richard and Philip N. Racine, eds. *The Fiery Trail: A Union Officer's Account of Sherman's Last Campaigns* by Thomas W. Osborn. Knoxville: University of Tennessee Press, 1986.

Hazen, William B. *A Narrative of Military Service*. Boston: Ticknor, 1885.

Headley, P.C. *Facing the Enemy, The Life and Military Career of Gen. William Tecumseh Sherman*. Boston: Lee and Shepard, 1865.

Hedley, Fenwick Y. *Marching through Georgia.* . . . Chicago: Donohoe, Henneberry, 1890.

Henken, Elissa R. "Taming the Enemy, Georgia Narratives About the Civil War," *Journal of Folklore Research* 40 (September-December 2003): 289-307.

Hirshon, Stanley P. *The White Tecumseh, A Biography of William T. Sherman.* New York: John Wiley, 1997.

Hitchcock, Henry M. *Marching with Sherman.* Edited by M.A. DeWolfe Howe. New Haven: Yale University Press, 1927.

Hughes, Nathaniel Cheairs, Jr. *General William J. Hardee, Old Reliable.* Baton Rouge: Louisiana State University Press, 1965.

Hughes, Nathaniel Cheairs, Jr. and Gordon D. Whitney. *Jefferson Davis in Blue, The Life of Sherman's Relentless Warrior.* Baton Rouge: Louisiana State University Press, 2002.

In Memoriam William T. Sherman. Proceedings of the Senate and Assembly of the State of New York . . . Albany, March 29, 1892. Albany, New York: James B. Lyon, 1892.

Jones, Archer. *Civil War Command and Strategy, The Process of Victory and Defeat.* New York: The Free Press, 1992.

Jones, Katherine M., ed. *When Sherman Came: Southern Women and the Great March.* Indianapolis: Bobbs-Merrill, 1964.

Kennett, Lee. *Marching Through Georgia, The Story of Soldiers & Civilians during Sherman's Campaign.* New York: Harper Collins, 1995.

_____. *Sherman, A Soldier's Life.* New York: Harper Collins, 2001.

Lewis, Lloyd. *Sherman, Fighting Prophet.* New York: Harcourt, Brace, 1932.

Liddell Hart, Basil H. *Sherman, Soldier, Realist, American.* New York: Frederick A. Praeger, 1929.

Marszalek, John F. *Commander of All Lincoln's Armies, a Life of Henry W. Halleck.* Cambridge: Harvard University Press, 2004.

_____. *Sherman's Other War, The General and the Civil War Press.* rev. ed. Kent, Ohio: Kent State University Press, 1999.

_____. *Sherman, A Soldier's Passion For Order.* New York: The Free Press, 1993.

Martin, Samuel J. *"Kill Cavalry" Sherman's Merchant of Terror: The Life of Union General Hugh Judson Kilpatrick.* Cranbury, New Jersey: Farleigh Dicknson University Press, 1996.

McCormick, Edgar L., Edward G. McGehee, and Mary Strahl, eds. *Sherman in Georgia. Selected Source Materials for College Research Papers.* General Editor Roland Bartel. Boston: D.C. Heath, 1961.

McKinney, Francis E. *Education in Violence: The Life of George H. Thomas and the History of the Army of the Cumberland.* Detroit: Wayne State University Press, 1961.

McNeill, William J. "A Survey of Confederate Soldier Morale During Sherman's Campaigns Through Georgia and the Carolinas," *Georgia Historical Quarterly* 55 (Spring 1971): 1-25.

Melton, Brian. "The Town That Sherman Wouldn't Burn. Sherman's March and Madison, Georgia in History, Memory, and Legend," *Georgia Historical Quarterly* 86 (Summer 2002): 201-30.

Miller, William Bluffton. "'We Have Surely Done A Big Work': The Diary of a Hoosier Soldier on Sherman's March to the Sea," ed. by Jeffrey L. Patrick and Robert Willey. *Indiana Magazine of History* 94 (September 1998): 214-39.

Neely, Mark E., Jr. "Was the Civil War A Total War?" *Civil War History* 37 (March 1991): 5-28.

Nevin, David. *Sherman's March: Atlanta to the Sea.* New York: Time-Life, 1986.

Nichols, George W. *The Story of the Great March from the Diary of a Staff Officer.* New York: Harper and Brothers, 1865.

Parks, Joseph H. *Joseph E. Brown of Georgia*. Baton Rouge: Louisiana State University Press, 1977.

Parrish, William E. *Frank Blair, Lincoln's Conservative*. Columbia: University of Missouri Press, 1998.

Pepper, George W. *Personal Recollections of Sherman's Campaign in Georgia and the Carolinas*. Zanesville, Ohio: Hugh Dunn, 1866.

Quarles, Benjamin. *The Negro in the Civil War*. Boston: Little Brown, 1953.

Rable, George C. *Civil Wars: Women and the Crisis of Southern Nationalism*. Urbana: University of Illinois Press, 1989.

Royster, Charles. *The Destructive War, William Tecumseh Sherman, Stonewall Jackson, and the Americans*. New York: Alfred A. Knopf, 1991.

Senour, F. *Major General William T. Sherman and His Campaigns*. Chicago: Henry M. Sherwood, 1865.

Sherman, William T. *General Sherman's Official Accounts of His Great March Through Georgia and the Carolinas*. New York: Bruce & Huntington, 1865.

_____. *Memoirs of General William T. Sherman*. New York: The Library of America, 1990.

Simpson, Brooks D. *Ulysses S. Grant, Triumph Over Adversity, 1822-1865*. New York: Houghton Mifflin, 2000.

Simpson, John Eddins. *Howell Cobb: the Politics of Ambition*. Chicago: Adams Press, 1973.

Slocum, Charles E. *Life and Services of Major General Henry Warner Slocum, Officer of the United States Army*. Toledo: Slocum, 1913.

Smith, Jean Edward. *Grant*. New York: Simon and Schuster, 2001.

Smith, Mark A. "Sherman's Unexpected Companions: Marching Through Georgia with Jomini and Clausewitz," *Georgia Historical Quarterly* 81 (Spring 1997): 1-24.

Sword, Wiley. *Embrace an Angry Wind: the Confederacy's Last*

Hurrah—Spring Hill, Franklin, and Nashville. New York: Harper Collins.

Thomas, Benjamin P. and Harold M. Hyman. *Stanton: the Life and Times of Lincoln's Secretary of War.* New York: Alfred A. Knopf, 1962.

Vetter, Charles E. "From Atlanta to Savanna, A Sociological Perspective of William T. Sherman's March Through Georgia," in Theodore P. Savas and David A. Woodbury, *The Campaign for Atlanta & Sherman's March to the Sea.* Campbell, California: Savas Woodbury, 1994, 375-412.

_____. *Sherman, Merchant of Terror, Advocate of Peace.* Gretna, Louisiana: Pelican, 1992.

Walters, John B. *Merchant of Terror, General Sherman and Total War.* Indianapolis: Bobbs-Merrill, 1973.

Wheeler, Richard. *Sherman's March.* New York: Harper Collins, 1978.

INDEX